THE ULTIMATE RPG QUEST KEEPER

A Journal to Keep Your Campaign Rolling

JEF ALDRICH & JON TAYLOR

ADAMS MEDIA

NEW YORK   LONDON   TORONTO   SYDNEY   NEW DELHI

Adams Media
An Imprint of Simon & Schuster, Inc.
100 Technology Center Drive
Stoughton, Massachusetts 02072

First Adams Media hardcover edition September 2021

ADAMS MEDIA and colophon are trademarks of Simon & Schuster.

For information about special discounts for bulk purchases, please contact Simon & Schuster Special Sales at 1-866-506-1949 or business@simonandschuster.com.

The Simon & Schuster Speakers Bureau can bring authors to your live event. For more information or to book an event contact the Simon & Schuster Speakers Bureau at 1-866-248-3049 or visit our website at www.simonspeakers.com.

Interior design by Julia Jacintho
Interior images © 123RF/pashabo; Getty Images/greyj

Manufactured in the United States of America

1 2021

ISBN 978-1-5072-1678-1

CONTENTS

CHARACTER FIVE ... 109

CHARACTER SIX ... 133

5

INTRODUCTION

When you pick up your dice and start your latest RPG on the road to adventure, an endless vista of possibilities awaits you. Each new person you meet, each battle you fight, the friends, foes, and treasures you discover along the way are shining lights along your path to role-playing immortality. It would truly be a shame if those details were to be lost to the impermanence of your memory. That's where *The Ultimate RPG Quest Keeper* comes in handy. Journaling the time your character spends in a game can be a truly rewarding way of building depth and discovering opportunities to expand your role-play in the future. Besides, it never hurts to have a record in case you forget the name of that one goblin with the eyepatch.

This book helps track all the information needed for your adventures. It's also your guide to determine what information is worth keeping hold of. Each chapter in this book is filled with prompts, tables, and suggestions that make it easy to take your character from bare numbers to a fleshed-out person. You'll also find plenty of space for notes, a great chance to put down your thoughts, impressions, suspicions, and just about anything that doesn't fit under any of the other options. Each section is primed to help you create a character as unique as you would hope.

Once you've crafted a chronicle that describes your character's personality, traits, and every other detail of backstory and history, you'll be able to use it as a resource. If you find yourself wondering what to say or how to act in a given role-play situation, just look to the pages here and inspiration will follow. Journaling is a great way to keep your character consistent and on-brand from one adventure to the next.

With space for ten characters' worth of information, you'll be able to bring this quest keeper from game to game and never feel like you're just playing some numbers on a sheet. You'll have a true detailed character who can breathe life into whatever setting you find yourself. And we all know that a fully developed character can slay more dragons, collect more treasure, and have more adventures!

HOW TO USE THIS BOOK

Using this book couldn't be simpler. First, choose a character: You can use this book for a character you're already playing, or start journaling when you create a new one. The options you'll find listed later in this book are intended to work for any genre you like, from sword-and-sorcery-style dungeon crawls to space adventures and cyberpunk narratives.

The second step is to put pen to paper. Start thinking like your character! Did they grow up wealthy or rough? How do they feel about the other folks they meet on a daily basis? Are they happy in general? Answering these sorts of questions can put you in the right mindset to unlock some incredible details and opportunities when you're playing later on, or just waxing nostalgic when revisiting campaigns from long ago.

Each section is set up with different ways to guide you toward making your character more than just what you've put on their character sheet. While we've certainly done as much as we can to populate the pages with as many options as possible, your character can always be more unusual than anything we could have anticipated; so we left some blank space in just about every prompt for you to go wild. While you certainly might be playing as a Human Fighter (and that's great!), we can't discount here that you won't be playing as a giant floating brain wearing an ironic trucker hat, or a crack in space-time that constantly pours forth ordinary-looking rats. So we've made allowances for everyone.

There are also some more free-form areas where you will be provided with a question as a prompt to help the creative juices flow. These allow you to give more detailed information about things that you might not cover so easily otherwise. Just thinking about these questions and what they mean to your character can spark ideas about their feelings toward a plethora of subjects. You can imagine their general inclination toward show tunes or the quality of the beds in any particular flea-bitten tavern.

The guidelines presented here don't need to be your character's entire story. As you invest time and care into your character and the world they inhabit, just writing about them—putting down your thoughts, feelings, and stories about your character—can contribute a richness to your experience and a sense of connection to your game.

CHARACTER ONE

....

Character Name

Remember, you can create a character any time, but it takes investment to make them yours. Spend some time thinking about your character—not only their appearance and gear, but also their backstory and their psychology. How will they react in a given situation? This is a great place to start.

CHARACTER NAME AND DESCRIPTION

To begin, you'll detail your character's name and appearance, which is what you'll reference when describing them to other players. Go big and be distinctive! The best characters are the most memorable, and bold decisions when building your look are a great place to begin. And remember: Just because you're starting your game doesn't mean your character only just popped into existence. A few nicknames, epithets, and quirks now will go a long way in the future.

CHARACTER NAME

What's in a name? Potential, for a start. Your character's name can say a lot about them, reflecting their parentage, species, nation, and calling, all while conveying brutality, beauty, or mystery.

Full Name: Epidem Shore

Known Aliases/Nicknames:

....

....

....

Titles Earned:

....

....

....

Draw your character here:

PLACE OF ORIGIN

Can folks tell where you hail from just by your gait or the cut of your hair? You might be a blank slate or wear your homeland on your sleeve like a badge. If you're looking for inspiration, consider a few of the keywords here.

Place of Origin Name:

....

Location Type:

- Plains
- Forest
- Tundra
- Coast
- City
- Settlement
- Island
- Swamp
- Hills
- Mountains
- Castle/Fort
- Plane
- Planet
- Colony
- ....
- ....

Location Description (check all that apply):

- Shimmering
- Battle-Ravaged
- Silent
- Fetid
- Noble
- Drowned
- Fae
- Calm
- Unsullied
- Stony
- Infested
- Pastoral
- Sunny
- Hardscrabble
- Enchanted
- Bustling
- Burning
- Eternal
- Vanishing
- Dead
- Broken
- Deep
- Whispering
- Forgotten
- Ruined
- Shadowy
- Windswept
- Verdant
- ....
- ....

PHYSICAL DESCRIPTION

You can convey a great deal about your character with little more than body language. Shy and slight, cloaked against the shadows? Or burly and imposing, rattling the ground you walk on? How do you make an impression without a word?

Species/Subspecies:

....

Height: ....

Weight: ....

Build: ....

Eye Color: ....

Body Texture:

- ▢ Skin
- ▢ Hair
- ▢ Fur
- ▢ Feather
- ▢ Scale
- ▢ ....
- ▢ ....

Coloring:

....

....

Other Defining Traits:

....

....

....

....

....

....

....

....

....

....

....

....

Defining Physical Traits:

▢ Battle Scar:

....

....

....

▢ War Wound:

....

....

....

▢ Striking Feature:

....

....

....

▢ Magical Mutation:

....

....

....

▢ Curious Affectation:

....

....

....

▢ Mystic Special Effects:

....

....

....

▢ Tattoos or Scarification:

....

....

....

▢ Bestial Attributes:

....

....

....

▢ Jewelry and Piercings:

....

....

....

PERSONALITY

What are the day-to-day attitudes that you bring to your party and your work? Are you fun to be around? Honest and headstrong? Select all that apply.

- Pleasant
- Angry
- Morose
- Forthright
- Flamboyant
- Quiet
- Kind

- Reserved
- Outgoing
- Proud
- Selfish
- Devious
- Clever
- Witty

- Guarded
- Trusting
- Suspicious
- Sunny
- Earnest
- Withdrawn
- Lazy

- Meticulous
- Overconfident
- Modest
- Caring
- Fun
- Pessimistic
- Candid

Do you get along well with your traveling companions?

....
....
....
....
....
....
....
....
....
....

How do you react to strangers and potential foes?

....
....
....
....
....
....
....
....
....
....

ADDITIONAL CHARACTER DESCRIPTION NOTES

....
....
....
....
....
....
....
....
....
....
....

HISTORY AND BACKSTORY

Here you'll put into words the past that you've left behind as your character steps forward into the larger world of the game. Does the past haunt you? Are you followed by the remnants of a life you long to escape? Or do you miss the simplicity of the days before you stepped out onto your road? By detailing your history, you provide a map of how you'll interact with the game world now and in the future.

FAMILY BACKGROUND

Everyone comes from somewhere, even if they technically come from no one. Use this space to list your family and their status.

Father's Name: ....

Father Is:

▢ Living   ▢ Deceased   ▢ Unknown

▢ ....
....

▢ ....
....

Mother's Name: ....

Mother Is:

▢ Living   ▢ Deceased   ▢ Unknown

▢ ....
....

▢ ....
....

Spouse/Partner Name:
....

Sibling Names and Birth Order:
....
....
....
....
....

Children/Grandchildren Names:
....
....
....
....
....

Other Family or Notable Figures' Names:
....
....
....
....

What influence did your family have on who you have become?
....
....
....
....
....
....
....
....

FAMILY DRAMA

A great way to build hooks and intrigue is to add some family drama that you've left behind or that still haunts you to this day. Check the list items that correspond with your character.

- A sibling fell to evil long ago. You still feel a sense of responsibility when their predation affects those you know.

- You were stolen away from a loving home as a babe and raised secretly for some evil purpose. You still wonder about your original family.

- You're next in line to the throne some-where, which explains why assassins keep showing up.

- Your parents were replaced by some-thing unnatural when you were small. Somehow you escaped, but you've been weary and perceptive ever since.

- You were raised by a family of another spe-cies, leaving you steeped in their culture and a little less comfortable in your own.

- You lost a great love once. You were even considering settling down. But they van-ished, and that loss still drives you.

- Your family is a long lineage of a sin-gle proud work, but you never had the hands or stomach for the family busi-ness. Perhaps they still resent you for abandoning the tradition.

- No childhood trauma befell you or your family. You grew up peacefully and happy, content with your parents and siblings around you. Several are still among us, and you visit them for a source of strength to this day.

- ....
  ....
  ....

WEALTH STATUS

Are you living the high life, or is a rougher path for you at the moment? For some adventurers, this answer can change with ease; they find themselves rolling high after a big score, then scrabble to pay for lodging while seeking out the next job. Here, focus on your character's ideal wealth status. Where on the social strata are they the most comfortable?

- **Contented Pauper:** Scruffy, rough, and cheap even in the best of times.

- **Lean Adventurer:** Always ready to head out; it's always been about the fights instead of the scores.

- **Easy Come, Easy Goer:** You rise to the level money can buy, sleeping in barns with the same comfort as luxury suites.

- **Canny Mercantilist:** Adventure is a second business to you, and you carry wares wherever you go, offering goods and services to towns as you cross them. As such, you're usually comfortable and can expect favorable service and rates from your fellow merchant peers.

- **Savvy Grifter:** You always seem to be comfortable as long as there are enough suckers and marks in the area. The speed of your smile and wit are bested only by the speed at which you leave town.

- **Scion of Success:** Maybe your pockets are empty at the moment, but every-one knows your family has full coffers. Given your vaunted status, it would be unseemly to sleep rough.

- **High Roller:** Money is as important to you as food and water. Even in hard times, you always seem to have the little extra amenities.

- ....
  ....
  ....

HEROIC BEGINNING

There comes a time in every hero's life when they must accept that they are no longer the person they were yesterday—that they can't go back. What did your moment look like? When you stepped out the door and into a larger world, was it voluntary, or were you pushed? In the following list, you'll find a few examples of common steps that take adventurers from an old life to a new one. Choose one or make up your own.

Marching to Battle: You signed up to defend your home, country, or way of life, and marched from home to war. Then you watched someone die and it changed everything.

Apprenticeship's End: It was a grueling education, but even more so an abrupt end, shoved out the door with nothing but the clothes on your back and the rudimentary tools of a trade. You returned home once, but it had vanished from the face of the world.

Local Hero: You weren't trained for it, but when doom befell your home, you rushed to help rather than cower and wait. Now you live for that same rush. However, you were struck by a dangerous curse.

Call of the Wild: You always felt more comfortable away from the smell and noise of the crowd, and the adventurer path gave you the freedom to live outside the walls. You fell in love along the path to adventure.

Last Survivor: You used to be happy, living among your kin in your hometown. But that's all gone now. Unmoored and hardened, you turned to a wandering life. Your simple journey became complicated as you mistakenly stepped into another world.

Lying Low: Your last job didn't go so well. It should've been a perfect score, but the guards had changed, or you didn't see that trap. Now, shamed and wanted, you can't go home, and need to get away with your skin. You found a mystic relic early on, and your fortunes have been shaped around it.

An Unexpected Meeting: You found someone or something in the shadows that offered you a bargain. A short-term job that seems to go on forever, or power at a price. You wonder if you should have said no. You lived when all signs, mystical or practical, suggest you should have died.

The Quest: You set out with a single mission burning in your heart. To vanquish one foe. To retrieve one relic. Perhaps you've yet to do so, or perhaps you've completed that mission, but there are always new quests. You found the first wanted poster with your face on it a day after you walked away from home.

MOTIVATIONS

At a primal level, something calls every adventurer and hero to action. Understanding what drives your character to venture forth every day can help you steer decisions over the course of the game. Choose one of these lists and mark which of the options applies to your character.

■ Looking out for the little guy

    ■ Used to be the little guy
    ■ Used to be the bully
    ■ Failed to defend someone in the past

    ■ ....

    ....

    ■ ....

    ....

■ Seeking fame and fortune

    ■ Left a hardscrabble existence on hope
    ■ Always felt big things were coming
    ■ Wants the world to know your name

    ■ ....

    ....

    ■ ....

    ....

■ Called to adventure by the gods

    ■ You've been chosen since childhood and groomed for this
    ■ Inspiration came in the form of a vision on the battlefield
    ■ You've sought out the forgiveness of the gods in atonement for a previous life of transgression

    ■ ....

    ....

    ■ ....

    ....

■ Avenging a wrong

    ■ It's a personal vendetta the world doesn't know about
    ■ You seek to stop a great evil that threatens all
    ■ You already avenged the wrong and are seeking new purpose

    ■ ....

    ....

    ■ ....

    ....

■ A perilous path to power

    ■ You've made a dark trade, and collection on your debt will come someday
    ■ The power you've attained came at a dire cost to your body and mind
    ■ You've left a trail of crimes behind you that you must always run from

    ■ ....

    ....

    ■ ....

    ....

■ Following your hero's footsteps

    ■ Your hero was the hero of your people— many follow in their footsteps; few succeed
    ■ Someone saved your life once, and you are compelled not to waste that gift
    ■ Your hero may have fallen but you have learned from their example all the same

    ■ ....

    ....

    ■ ....

    ....

ADDITIONAL HISTORY
AND BACKSTORY NOTES

Following a trusted friend

- Childhood friends for life
- Your mentor vanished, leaving only cryptic clues
- The spirit of a fallen compatriot spurs you onward
- ....
- ....

Displaced from home

- You still hold a grudge against those who destroyed your old life
- You were separated from your home by disaster
- You earned your banishment and bear that shame
- ....
- ....

Trained for combat but the war is over

- Selling your sword arm beats life on the farm
- The war may be over but you haven't forgotten or forgiven
- You developed a taste for conflict and seek it out to this day
- ....
- ....

GEAR AND OTHER ITEMS OF INTEREST

Whether you're considering the basics, like fifty feet of silken rope plus flint and tinder, or the truly unique, like the enchanted eye of the last green dragon or a hot-rodded custom starfighter, the trappings you carry around convey a story, and that story can be as simple or as complex as your own history. In this section, list your weapons, equipment, and miscellaneous items you possess or have decided to bring with you.

GEAR

Consider the general state of your belongings. Are you a fastidious adventurer who keeps each item organized, clean, and in good working order? Do you let things fall into messy disrepair, counting on good fortune and jerry-rigging to keep your tools useful?

Weapons

Did you begin your adventuring career with the only weapon you'll ever need? A trusted heirloom or sainted magic relic that will see you through all hardship? Or do you replace weapons with the ease of breathing, always seeking the next upgrade? Here, you'll detail your favorite weapons and your relationship to them.

Secondary Weapons

Even the most stringent devotee to the arts of the blade may carry more than one weapon, just in case. Here, list any other weapons you carry or have gathered on the journey.

Weapon (circle one)	Name	Model	Stats and Bonuses	History
primary secondary				
primary secondary				
primary secondary				
primary secondary				
primary secondary				
primary secondary				
primary secondary				

Gear Goals

It's not often that you get the chance to start the game with everything you want, and it doesn't matter if your target is something you need for quest purposes or just a wizard staff you happen to think looks particularly good with your current hat: A large part of adventuring is heading out to get what you want. So, think about just that: what you want. This space can serve as a reminder, a wish list for an interested game master (GM), or just a set of goals to put out in the world.

Item	Description	Probable Location

Gear Relationship

- Nothing but the weapons and the clothes on your back
- Packed for emergencies
- Packed for comfort
- Prepared for everything
- Compulsive collector
- ....

Storage Style

- Organized
- Untidy
- Stored in pouches and straps
- Carried by underlings
- Stored in otherspace
- Kept in the saddlebags
- Hidden on yourself
- ....

Gear Appearance

- Neglected
- Piecemeal
- Rusted
- Stolen
- Handcrafted
- Heirloom
- Store-bought
- Polished
- Customized
- Mystical
- ....

TREASURED BELONGINGS

There's always room on your character sheet for the basics, but not every piece of equipment you're carrying is basic. Here you can list the things that have real significance and importance, whether that be to the campaign at large or just to you. Whether it's as simple as a locket with a photo or as epic as the only rock left of your demolished home world, certain items are just more important.

Item:	
Description	**Origin**
	▨ Birthright ▨ Crafted ▨ Claimed ▨ Reward ▨ Discovered ▨ Other: ▨ Stole .... ▨ Purchased ....

Item:	
Description	**Origin**
	▨ Birthright ▨ Crafted ▨ Claimed ▨ Reward ▨ Discovered ▨ Other: ▨ Stole .... ▨ Purchased ....

Item:	
Description	**Origin**
	▨ Birthright ▨ Crafted ▨ Claimed ▨ Reward ▨ Discovered ▨ Other: ▨ Stole .... ▨ Purchased ....

Item:

Description	Origin
	▨ Birthright ▨ Crafted ▨ Claimed ▨ Reward ▨ Discovered ▨ Other: ▨ Stole .... ▨ Purchased ....

Item:

Description	Origin
	▨ Birthright ▨ Crafted ▨ Claimed ▨ Reward ▨ Discovered ▨ Other: ▨ Stole .... ▨ Purchased ....

Item:

Description	Origin
	▨ Birthright ▨ Crafted ▨ Claimed ▨ Reward ▨ Discovered ▨ Other: ▨ Stole .... ▨ Purchased ....

Item:

Description	Origin
	▨ Birthright ▨ Crafted ▨ Claimed ▨ Reward ▨ Discovered ▨ Other: ▨ Stole .... ▨ Purchased ....

PROPERTY

Have you come into possession of something large enough that it requires titles and deeds, as well as maintenance or even a constant staff for upkeep? Perhaps a secret lair, an office for your paranormal investigations, a starcruiser, or a beat-up car that'll get from point A to B if you baby it enough? When you take ownership of conveyance or property, record it here.

Property Type:

- Vehicle/Steed
- Home
- Business
- Town/City
- Kingdom
- Country
- Planet
- ....
- ....

Property Location: ....
....
....

Description: ....
....
....

Condition: ....
....
....

Property Type:

- Vehicle/Steed
- Home
- Business
- Town/City
- Kingdom
- Country
- Planet
- ....
- ....

Property Location: ....
....
....

Description: ....
....
....

Condition: ....
....
....

ADDITIONAL ITEM NOTES

26

ABILITIES OF NOTE

As you progress through your game world, you'll become ever more competent at your chosen field(s). Warriors become stronger and more tactically capable; casters add an ever-increasing array of arcane and divine tricks to their arsenal; negotiators become increasingly versed in matters of diplomacy and discussion; and so on. Here you'll record a list of your most efficacious and incredible abilities, along with notes describing how you personalize them to make them truly yours.

SIGNATURE ABILITIES

A perfect blade swing that can cut through the air itself. A softly spoken word that can divert the course of an empire. A granted miracle that calls down heaven itself to cast away the dead. Many characters will come to be known for such incredible feats, and those signature techniques they have will bear their names into legend.

Skill Name:	■ Physical ■ Divine ■ Technological ■ Mental ■ Social ■ .... ■ Magical ■ Artifact ■		
Skill Effect:	Personal Upgrades:		Element Change:
Increased Range:	Increased Power:		Visual Special Effects:

Power Source (check one):

■ Innate:	■ Taught:	■ Bestowed:
■ Upgrade:	■ Other:	■ Other:

Skill Name:	▢ Physical ▢ Divine ▢ Technological
	▢ Mental ▢ Social ▢
	▢ Magical ▢ Artifact ▢

Skill Effect:	Personal Upgrades:	Element Change:

Increased Range:	Increased Power:	Visual Special Effects:

Power Source (check one):

▢ Innate:	▢ Taught:	▢ Bestowed:
▢ Upgrade:	▢ Other:	▢ Other:

Skill Name:	▢ Physical ▢ Divine ▢ Technological
	▢ Mental ▢ Social ▢
	▢ Magical ▢ Artifact ▢

Skill Effect:	Personal Upgrades:	Element Change:

Increased Range:	Increased Power:	Visual Special Effects:

Power Source (check one):

▢ Innate:	▢ Taught:	▢ Bestowed:
▢ Upgrade:	▢ Other:	▢ Other:

COMPLETE TOOL KIT

Adventurers may make their legacy on the flash and drama of their most powerful tools, but they survive long enough to earn that legacy through growth and maintenance of a suite of survival, combat, and social tools ranging from beginners' survival tools to expert techniques.

Skill Name:	Skill Name:	Skill Name:	Skill Name:	Skill Name:
....	....	....	....	....
Type:	Type:	Type:	Type:	Type:
▦ Technique	▦ Technique	▦ Technique	▦ Technique	▦ Technique
▦ Spell	▦ Spell	▦ Spell	▦ Spell	▦ Spell
▦ Power	▦ Power	▦ Power	▦ Power	▦ Power
▦	▦	▦	▦	▦ ....
▦	▦	▦	▦	▦ ....
Description	**Description**	**Description**	**Description**	**Description**
Stats and Bonuses	**Stats and Bonuses**	**Stats and Bonuses**	**Stats and Bonuses**	**Stats and Bonuses**
Special Effects	**Special Effects**	**Special Effects**	**Special Effects**	**Special Effects**

NON-PLAYER CHARACTERS

Nobody goes through life without making some connections with the people around them, and your character should be no different. Whether it's someone you consider as close to you as a member of your own family, or a simple shop owner that you know has the best prices in town, these are the folks around you that mean the most.

CHARACTER

Character Name: ....

Character Type:

- ▨ Government Official/Politician
- ▨ Business Owner
- ▨ Family Member
- ▨ Non-Party Adventurer
- ▨ Faction or Gang Leader
- ▨ Guard/Soldier
- ▨ Refugee/Person in Need
- ▨ Old Friend
- ▨ Teacher/Expert
- ▨ Monster
- ▨ Courier
- ▨ Child/Youth
- ▨ Extraplanar/Extraplanetary Visitor
- ▨ ....
- ▨ ....

Relationship:

- ▨ Friendly
- ▨ Transactional
- ▨ Competitive
- ▨ Adversarial
- ▨ Violent
- ▨ ....
- ▨ ....

Physical Description: ....
....
....
....
....

Character Personality:

- ▨ Shifty. Paranoid. Always looking around.
- ▨ Boisterous. Welcoming. Calls you "friend."
- ▨ Serious. All business. No sense of humor.
- ▨ Friendly. Gentle. Likes being helpful.
- ▨ Cowardly. Whiny. Hates being called on.
- ▨ Gruff. Grumpy. Grudgingly does business with you.
- ▨ Greedy. Slick. In it for the profit.
- ▨ Flirty. Charming. Makes you feel special.
- ▨ Bombastic. Dramatic. All eyes on them.
- ▨ ....
- ▨ ....
- ▨ ....
- ▨ ....

What They Can Do for You:

- ▨ Has your back in any adventure
- ▨ Provides mentorship and guidance
- ▨ Boosts your ego with praise and admiration
- ▨ Always has the latest gossip
- ▨ Buys or sells contraband and rare items
- ▨ Knows when big crimes are happening
- ▨ Can introduce you to people you need
- ▨ Sells discounted goods
- ▨ Owes you an undetermined favor
- ▨ Gives you a place to crash and lie low
- ▨ Can get you the information you need
- ▨ Gets anything/anyone where it needs to go
- ▨ ....
- ▨ ....
- ▨ ....
- ▨ ....

OTHER CHARACTERS OF NOTE

There are plenty of people in the world that you hear of but don't directly interact with. The name of the local governor that might come in handy lately. The employer who sent you on your latest job. Even the bartender at your favorite hangout might be worth remembering and coming back to. Feel free to jot down anyone that feels important to remember.

ADDITIONAL NPC NOTES

CAMPAIGN NOTES

Herein lies your opportunity to record the great (and the infamous) deeds of your character and their journey. As they grow in power and glory, you'll be able to document each slain foe and each well-met hero on your road, and reflect back on the early days of your starting career. Additionally, it never hurts to keep a record, in case you forget an important name or person who will assuredly crop up later.

PARTY MEMBERS

It's rare that you'll venture forth to adventure alone. Who watches your back? Do you trust them implicitly or do you keep one eye open? You can list the important events and interactions here, or note down the small details to call up again when role-playing in the future.

IMPORTANT EVENTS

How have you made your mark on the world? When the lyricists compose your ode, what stories will they lean on, and what dark paths and mistakes will they carefully elide? Be sure to mention the people you met along the way too, since you never know when they'll turn up again.

BATTLES

There's certainly no reason you can't use this section as a hunting journal or scoreboard, simply listing the types and vitals of every orc or space bug you dispatch. But you might also want to focus on the epic events, the villains that brought you to the edge of doom, or the moments of good fortune or tactical brilliance that make the best boastful brags.

Battle:	Notable Foes	Treasure Acquired
Resolution: ☐ Victory ☐ Defeat ☐ .... ☐	Notes and Details	

Battle:	Notable Foes	Treasure Acquired
Resolution: ☐ Victory ☐ Defeat ☐ .... ☐	Notes and Details	

Battle:	Notable Foes	Treasure Acquired
Resolution: ☐ Victory ☐ Defeat ☐ .... ☐	Notes and Details	

Battle:	Notable Foes	Treasure Acquired
Resolution: ▪ Victory ▪ Defeat ▪ .... ▪		
	Notes and Details	

Battle:	Notable Foes	Treasure Acquired
Resolution: ▪ Victory ▪ Defeat ▪ .... ▪		
	Notes and Details	

Battle:	Notable Foes	Treasure Acquired
Resolution: ▪ Victory ▪ Defeat ▪ .... ▪		
	Notes and Details	

ENCOUNTERS

Not every obstacle on your journey can or will be resolved at the edge of a blade. You might perform some great feat of diplomacy, explore a new and undiscovered land, meet some of the luminaries and famous warriors of your world, or encounter any number of other incredible experiences.

ADDITIONAL CAMPAIGN NOTES

CHARACTER TWO

Character Name

Remember, you can create a character any time, but it takes investment to make them yours. Spend some time thinking about your character—not only their appearance and gear, but also their backstory and their psychology. How will they react in a given situation? This is a great place to start.

CHARACTER NAME AND DESCRIPTION

To begin, you'll detail your character's name and appearance, which is what you'll reference when describing them to other players. Go big and be distinctive! The best characters are the most memorable, and bold decisions when building your look are a great place to begin. And remember: Just because you're starting your game doesn't mean your character only just popped into existence. A few nicknames, epithets, and quirks now will go a long way in the future.

CHARACTER NAME

What's in a name? Potential, for a start. Your character's name can say a lot about them, reflecting their parentage, species, nation, and calling, all while conveying brutality, beauty, or mystery.

Full Name: *Xekiel Locke*

Known Aliases/Nicknames:

....
....
....

Titles Earned:

....
....
....

Draw your character here:

PLACE OF ORIGIN

Can folks tell where you hail from just by your gait or the cut of your hair? You might be a blank slate or wear your homeland on your sleeve like a badge. If you're looking for inspiration, consider a few of the keywords here.

Place of Origin Name:

....

Location Type:

- Plains
- Forest
- Tundra
- Coast
- City
- Settlement
- Island
- Swamp
- Hills
- Mountains
- Castle/Fort
- Plane
- Planet
- Colony
- ....
- ....

Location Description
(check all that apply):

- Shimmering
- Battle-Ravaged
- Silent
- Fetid
- Noble

- Drowned
- Fae
- Calm
- Unsullied
- Stony
- Infested
- Pastoral
- Sunny
- Hardscrabble
- Enchanted
- Bustling
- Burning
- Eternal
- Vanishing
- Dead
- Broken
- Deep
- Whispering
- Forgotten
- Ruined
- Shadowy
- Windswept
- Verdant
- ....
- ....

PHYSICAL DESCRIPTION

You can convey a great deal about your character with little more than body language. Shy and slight, cloaked against the shadows? Or burly and imposing, rattling the ground you walk on? How do you make an impression without a word?

Species/Subspecies:

....

Height: ....

Weight: ....

Build: ....

Eye Color: ....

Body Texture:

- Skin
- Hair
- Fur
- Feather
- Scale
- ....
- ....

Coloring:

....

....

Other Defining Traits:

....

....

....

....

....

....

....

....

....

....

Defining Physical Traits:

- Battle Scar:

....

....

....

- War Wound:

....

....

....

- Striking Feature:

....

....

....

- Magical Mutation:

....

....

....

- Curious Affectation:

....

....

....

- Mystic Special Effects:

....

....

....

- Tattoos or Scarification:

....

....

....

- Bestial Attributes:

....

....

....

- Jewelry and Piercings:

....

....

....

PERSONALITY

What are the day-to-day attitudes that you bring to your party and your work? Are you fun to be around? Honest and headstrong? Select all that apply.

- Pleasant
- Angry
- Morose
- Forthright
- Flamboyant
- Quiet
- Kind

- Reserved
- Outgoing
- Proud
- Selfish
- Devious
- Clever
- Witty

- Guarded
- Trusting
- Suspicious
- Sunny
- Earnest
- Withdrawn
- Lazy

- Meticulous
- Overconfident
- Modest
- Caring
- Fun
- Pessimistic
- Candid

Do you get along well with your traveling companions?

....

....

....

....

....

....

....

....

....

How do you react to strangers and potential foes?

....

....

....

....

....

....

....

....

....

ADDITIONAL CHARACTER DESCRIPTION NOTES

....

....

....

....

....

....

....

....

....

....

HISTORY AND BACKSTORY

Here you'll put into words the past that you've left behind as your character steps forward into the larger world of the game. Does the past haunt you? Are you followed by the remnants of a life you long to escape? Or do you miss the simplicity of the days before you stepped out onto your road? By detailing your history, you provide a map of how you'll interact with the game world now and in the future.

FAMILY BACKGROUND

Everyone comes from somewhere, even if they technically come from no one. Use this space to list your family and their status.

Father's Name: ....

Father Is:

■ Living ■ Deceased ■ Unknown

■ ....

....

■ ....

....

Mother's Name: ....

Mother Is:

■ Living ■ Deceased ■ Unknown

■ ....

....

■ ....

....

Spouse/Partner Name:

....

Sibling Names and Birth Order:

....

....

....

....

Children/Grandchildren Names:

....

....

....

....

....

....

....

Other Family or Notable Figures' Names:

....

....

....

....

....

What influence did your family have on who you have become?

....

....

....

....

....

....

....

....

FAMILY DRAMA

A great way to build hooks and intrigue is to add some family drama that you've left behind or that still haunts you to this day. Check the list items that correspond with your character.

- A sibling fell to evil long ago. You still feel a sense of responsibility when their predation affects those you know.

- You were stolen away from a loving home as a babe and raised secretly for some evil purpose. You still wonder about your original family.

- You're next in line to the throne some-where, which explains why assassins keep showing up.

- Your parents were replaced by some-thing unnatural when you were small. Somehow you escaped, but you've been weary and perceptive ever since.

- You were raised by a family of another spe-cies, leaving you steeped in their culture and a little less comfortable in your own.

- You lost a great love once. You were even considering settling down. But they van-ished, and that loss still drives you.

- Your family is a long lineage of a sin-gle proud work, but you never had the hands or stomach for the family busi-ness. Perhaps they still resent you for abandoning the tradition.

- No childhood trauma befell you or your family. You grew up peacefully and happy, content with your parents and siblings around you. Several are still among us, and you visit them for a source of strength to this day.

- ....
....
....

WEALTH STATUS

Are you living the high life, or is a rougher path for you at the moment? For some adventurers, this answer can change with ease; they find themselves rolling high after a big score, then scrabble to pay for lodging while seeking out the next job. Here, focus on your character's ideal wealth status. Where on the social strata are they the most comfortable?

- **Contented Pauper:** Scruffy, rough, and cheap even in the best of times.

- **Lean Adventurer:** Always ready to head out; it's always been about the fights instead of the scores.

- **Easy Come, Easy Goer:** You rise to the level money can buy, sleeping in barns with the same comfort as luxury suites.

- **Canny Mercantilist:** Adventure is a second business to you, and you carry wares wherever you go, offering goods and services to towns as you cross them. As such, you're usually comfortable and can expect favorable service and rates from your fellow merchant peers.

- **Savvy Grifter:** You always seem to be comfortable as long as there are enough suckers and marks in the area. The speed of your smile and wit are bested only by the speed at which you leave town.

- **Scion of Success:** Maybe your pockets are empty at the moment, but every-one knows your family has full coffers. Given your vaunted status, it would be unseemly to sleep rough.

- **High Roller:** Money is as important to you as food and water. Even in hard times, you always seem to have the little extra amenities.

- ....
....
....

HEROIC BEGINNING

There comes a time in every hero's life when they must accept that they are no longer the person they were yesterday—that they can't go back. What did your moment look like? When you stepped out the door and into a larger world, was it voluntary, or were you pushed? In the following list, you'll find a few examples of common steps that take adventurers from an old life to a new one. Choose one or make up your own.

- **Marching to Battle:** You signed up to defend your home, country, or way of life, and marched from home to war. Then you watched someone die and it changed everything.

- **Apprenticeship's End:** It was a grueling education, but even more so an abrupt end, shoved out the door with nothing but the clothes on your back and the rudimentary tools of a trade. You returned home once, but it had vanished from the face of the world.

- **Local Hero:** You weren't trained for it, but when doom befell your home, you rushed to help rather than cower and wait. Now you live for that same rush. However, you were struck by a dangerous curse.

- **Call of the Wild:** You always felt more comfortable away from the smell and noise of the crowd, and the adventurer path gave you the freedom to live outside the walls. You fell in love along the path to adventure.

- **Last Survivor:** You used to be happy, living among your kin in your hometown. But that's all gone now. Unmoored and hardened, you turned to a wandering life. Your simple journey became complicated as you mistakenly stepped into another world.

- **Lying Low:** Your last job didn't go so well. It should've been a perfect score, but the guards had changed, or you didn't see that trap. Now, shamed and wanted, you can't go home, and need to get away with your skin. You found a mystic relic early on, and your fortunes have been shaped around it.

- **An Unexpected Meeting:** You found someone or something in the shadows that offered you a bargain. A short-term job that seems to go on forever, or power at a price. You wonder if you should have said no. You lived when all signs, mystical or practical, suggest you should have died.

- **The Quest:** You set out with a single mission burning in your heart. To vanquish one foe. To retrieve one relic. Perhaps you've yet to do so, or perhaps you've completed that mission, but there are always new quests. You found the first wanted poster with your face on it a day after you walked away from home.

....
....
....
....
....
....
....
....
....
....
....
....
....
....

MOTIVATIONS

At a primal level, something calls every adventurer and hero to action. Understanding what drives your character to venture forth every day can help you steer decisions over the course of the game. Choose one of these lists and mark which of the options applies to your character.

Looking out for the little guy

- Used to be the little guy
- Used to be the bully
- Failed to defend someone in the past
- ....
  ....
- ....
  ....

Seeking fame and fortune

- Left a hardscrabble existence on hope
- Always felt big things were coming
- Wants the world to know your name
- ....
  ....
- ....
  ....

Called to adventure by the gods

- You've been chosen since childhood and groomed for this
- Inspiration came in the form of a vision on the battlefield
- You've sought out the forgiveness of the gods in atonement for a previous life of transgression
- ....
  ....
- ....
  ....

Avenging a wrong

- It's a personal vendetta the world doesn't know about
- You seek to stop a great evil that threatens all
- You already avenged the wrong and are seeking new purpose
- ....
  ....
- ....
  ....

A perilous path to power

- You've made a dark trade, and collection on your debt will come someday
- The power you've attained came at a dire cost to your body and mind
- You've left a trail of crimes behind you that you must always run from
- ....
  ....
- ....
  ....

Following your hero's footsteps

- Your hero was the hero of your people—many follow in their footsteps; few succeed
- Someone saved your life once, and you are compelled not to waste that gift
- Your hero may have fallen but you have learned from their example all the same
- ....
  ....
- ....
  ....

ADDITIONAL HISTORY AND BACKSTORY NOTES

Following a trusted friend

- Childhood friends for life
- Your mentor vanished, leaving only cryptic clues
- The spirit of a fallen compatriot spurs you onward
- ....
- ....

Displaced from home

- You still hold a grudge against those who destroyed your old life
- You were separated from your home by disaster
- You earned your banishment and bear that shame
- ....
- ....

Trained for combat but the war is over

- Selling your sword arm beats life on the farm
- The war may be over but you haven't forgotten or forgiven
- You developed a taste for conflict and seek it out to this day
- ....
- ....

GEAR AND OTHER ITEMS OF INTEREST

Whether you're considering the basics, like fifty feet of silken rope plus flint and tinder, or the truly unique, like the enchanted eye of the last green dragon or a hot-rodded custom starfighter, the trappings you carry around convey a story, and that story can be as simple or as complex as your own history. In this section, list your weapons, equipment, and miscellaneous items you possess or have decided to bring with you.

GEAR

Consider the general state of your belongings. Are you a fastidious adventurer who keeps each item organized, clean, and in good working order? Do you let things fall into messy disrepair, counting on good fortune and jerry-rigging to keep your tools useful?

Weapons

Did you begin your adventuring career with the only weapon you'll ever need? A trusted heirloom or sainted magic relic that will see you through all hardship? Or do you replace weapons with the ease of breathing, always seeking the next upgrade? Here, you'll detail your favorite weapons and your relationship to them.

Secondary Weapons

Even the most stringent devotee to the arts of the blade may carry more than one weapon, just in case. Here, list any other weapons you carry or have gathered on the journey.

Weapon (circle one)	Name	Model	Stats and Bonuses	History
primary secondary				
primary secondary				
primary secondary				
primary secondary				
primary secondary				
primary secondary				
primary secondary				

Gear Goals

It's not often that you get the chance to start the game with everything you want, and it doesn't matter if your target is something you need for quest purposes or just a wizard staff you happen to think looks particularly good with your current hat: A large part of adventuring is heading out to get what you want. So, think about just that: what you want. This space can serve as a reminder, a wish list for an interested game master (GM), or just a set of goals to put out in the world.

Item	Description	Probable Location

Gear Relationship

- Nothing but the weapons and the clothes on your back
- Packed for emergencies
- Packed for comfort
- Prepared for everything
- Compulsive collector
- ....

Storage Style

- Organized
- Untidy
- Stored in pouches and straps
- Carried by underlings
- Stored in otherspace
- Kept in the saddlebags
- Hidden on yourself
- ....

Gear Appearance

- Neglected
- Piecemeal
- Rusted
- Stolen
- Handcrafted
- Heirloom
- Store-bought
- Polished
- Customized
- Mystical
- ....

TREASURED BELONGINGS

There's always room on your character sheet for the basics, but not every piece of equipment you're carrying is basic. Here you can list the things that have real significance and importance, whether that be to the campaign at large or just to you. Whether it's as simple as a locket with a photo or as epic as the only rock left of your demolished home world, certain items are just more important.

Item:	
Description	**Origin**
	▨ Birthright ▨ Crafted ▨ Claimed ▨ Reward ▨ Discovered ▨ Other: ▨ Stole .... ▨ Purchased ....

Item:	
Description	**Origin**
	▨ Birthright ▨ Crafted ▨ Claimed ▨ Reward ▨ Discovered ▨ Other: ▨ Stole .... ▨ Purchased ....

Item:	
Description	**Origin**
	▨ Birthright ▨ Crafted ▨ Claimed ▨ Reward ▨ Discovered ▨ Other: ▨ Stole .... ▨ Purchased ....

Item:	
Description	**Origin**
	▨ Birthright ▨ Crafted ▨ Claimed ▨ Reward ▨ Discovered ▨ Other: ▨ Stole .... ▨ Purchased ....

Item:	
Description	**Origin**
	▨ Birthright ▨ Crafted ▨ Claimed ▨ Reward ▨ Discovered ▨ Other: ▨ Stole .... ▨ Purchased ....

Item:	
Description	**Origin**
	▨ Birthright ▨ Crafted ▨ Claimed ▨ Reward ▨ Discovered ▨ Other: ▨ Stole .... ▨ Purchased ....

Item:	
Description	**Origin**
	▨ Birthright ▨ Crafted ▨ Claimed ▨ Reward ▨ Discovered ▨ Other: ▨ Stole .... ▨ Purchased ....

PROPERTY

Have you come into possession of something large enough that it requires titles and deeds, as well as maintenance or even a constant staff for upkeep? Perhaps a secret lair, an office for your paranormal investigations, a starcruiser, or a beat-up car that'll get from point A to B if you baby it enough? When you take ownership of conveyance or property, record it here.

Property Type:

- ▨ Vehicle/Steed
- ▨ Home
- ▨ Business
- ▨ Town/City
- ▨ Kingdom
- ▨ Country
- ▨ Planet
- ▨ ....
- ▨ ....

Property Location: ....
....
....

Description: ....
....
....

Condition: ....
....
....

Property Type:

- ▨ Vehicle/Steed
- ▨ Home
- ▨ Business
- ▨ Town/City
- ▨ Kingdom
- ▨ Country
- ▨ Planet
- ▨ ....
- ▨ ....

Property Location: ....
....
....

Description: ....
....
....

Condition: ....
....
....

ADDITIONAL ITEM NOTES

....
....
....
....
....
....
....
....
....
....
....
....
....
....
....
....
....
....
....
....
....
....
....
....
....
....
....
....
....
....
....
....
....
....
....
....
....
....

ABILITIES OF NOTE

As you progress through your game world, you'll become ever more competent at your chosen field(s). Warriors become stronger and more tactically capable; casters add an ever-increasing array of arcane and divine tricks to their arsenal; negotiators become increasingly versed in matters of diplomacy and discussion; and so on. Here you'll record a list of your most efficacious and incredible abilities, along with notes describing how you personalize them to make them truly yours.

SIGNATURE ABILITIES

A perfect blade swing that can cut through the air itself. A softly spoken word that can divert the course of an empire. A granted miracle that calls down heaven itself to cast away the dead. Many characters will come to be known for such incredible feats, and those signature techniques they have will bear their names into legend.

Skill Name:	■ Physical ■ Divine ■ Technological ■ Mental ■ Social ■ .... ■ Magical ■ Artifact ■		
Skill Effect:	Personal Upgrades:		Element Change:
Increased Range:	Increased Power:		Visual Special Effects:
Power Source (check one):			
■ Innate:	■ Taught:		■ Bestowed:
■ Upgrade:	■ Other:		■ Other:

Skill Name:	☐ Physical ☐ Divine ☐ Technological
	☐ Mental ☐ Social ☐ ....
	☐ Magical ☐ Artifact ☐ ....

Skill Effect:	Personal Upgrades:	Element Change:

Increased Range:	Increased Power:	Visual Special Effects:

Power Source (check one):

☐ Innate:	☐ Taught:	☐ Bestowed:
☐ Upgrade:	☐ Other:	☐ Other:

Skill Name:	☐ Physical ☐ Divine ☐ Technological
	☐ Mental ☐ Social ☐ ....
	☐ Magical ☐ Artifact ☐ ....

Skill Effect:	Personal Upgrades:	Element Change:

Increased Range:	Increased Power:	Visual Special Effects:

Power Source (check one):

☐ Innate:	☐ Taught:	☐ Bestowed:
☐ Upgrade:	☐ Other:	☐ Other:

52

COMPLETE TOOL KIT

Adventurers may make their legacy on the flash and drama of their most powerful tools, but they survive long enough to earn that legacy through growth and maintenance of a suite of survival, combat, and social tools ranging from beginners' survival tools to expert techniques.

Skill Name:	Skill Name:	Skill Name:	Skill Name:	Skill Name:
Type:	Type:	Type:	Type:	Type:
▢ Technique ▢ Spell ▢ Power ▢ .... ▢	▢ Technique ▢ Spell ▢ Power ▢ .... ▢	▢ Technique ▢ Spell ▢ Power ▢ .... ▢	▢ Technique ▢ Spell ▢ Power ▢ .... ▢	▢ Technique ▢ Spell ▢ Power ▢ .... ▢ ....
Description	**Description**	**Description**	**Description**	**Description**
Stats and Bonuses	**Stats and Bonuses**	**Stats and Bonuses**	**Stats and Bonuses**	**Stats and Bonuses**
Special Effects	**Special Effects**	**Special Effects**	**Special Effects**	**Special Effects**

NON-PLAYER CHARACTERS

Nobody goes through life without making some connections with the people around them, and your character should be no different. Whether it's someone you consider as close to you as a member of your own family, or a simple shop owner that you know has the best prices in town, these are the folks around you that mean the most.

CHARACTER

Character Name: ....

Character Type:

- Government Official/Politician
- Business Owner
- Family Member
- Non-Party Adventurer
- Faction or Gang Leader
- Guard/Soldier
- Refugee/Person in Need
- Old Friend
- Teacher/Expert
- Monster
- Courier
- Child/Youth
- Extraplanar/Extraplanetary Visitor
- ....
- ....

Relationship:

- Friendly
- Transactional
- Competitive
- Adversarial
- Violent
- ....
- ....

Physical Description: ....

....
....
....
....
....

Character Personality:

- Shifty. Paranoid. Always looking around.
- Boisterous. Welcoming. Calls you "friend."
- Serious. All business. No sense of humor.
- Friendly. Gentle. Likes being helpful.
- Cowardly. Whiny. Hates being called on.
- Gruff. Grumpy. Grudgingly does business with you.
- Greedy. Slick. In it for the profit.
- Flirty. Charming. Makes you feel special.
- Bombastic. Dramatic. All eyes on them.
- ....
- ....
- ....
- ....

What They Can Do for You:

- Has your back in any adventure
- Provides mentorship and guidance
- Boosts your ego with praise and admiration
- Always has the latest gossip
- Buys or sells contraband and rare items
- Knows when big crimes are happening
- Can introduce you to people you need
- Sells discounted goods
- Owes you an undetermined favor
- Gives you a place to crash and lie low
- Can get you the information you need
- Gets anything/anyone where it needs to go
- ....
- ....
- ....
- ....

OTHER CHARACTERS OF NOTE

There are plenty of people in the world that you hear of but don't directly interact with. The name of the local governor that might come in handy lately. The employer who sent you on your latest job. Even the bartender at your favorite hangout might be worth remembering and coming back to. Feel free to jot down anyone that feels important to remember.

ADDITIONAL NPC NOTES

CAMPAIGN NOTES

Herein lies your opportunity to record the great (and the infamous) deeds of your character and their journey. As they grow in power and glory, you'll be able to document each slain foe and each well-met hero on your road, and reflect back on the early days of your starting career. Additionally, it never hurts to keep a record, in case you forget an important name or person who will assuredly crop up later.

PARTY MEMBERS

It's rare that you'll venture forth to adventure alone. Who watches your back? Do you trust them implicitly or do you keep one eye open? You can list the important events and interactions here, or note down the small details to call up again when role-playing in the future.

....
....
....
....
....
....
....
....
....
....
....
....
....
....
....
....
....
....
....
....
....

IMPORTANT EVENTS

How have you made your mark on the world? When the lyricists compose your ode, what stories will they lean on, and what dark paths and mistakes will they carefully elide? Be sure to mention the people you met along the way too, since you never know when they'll turn up again.

....
....
....
....
....
....
....
....
....
....
....
....
....
....
....
....
....
....
....
....

BATTLES

There's certainly no reason you can't use this section as a hunting journal or scoreboard, simply listing the types and vitals of every orc or space bug you dispatch. But you might also want to focus on the epic events, the villains that brought you to the edge of doom, or the moments of good fortune or tactical brilliance that make the best boastful brags.

Battle:	Notable Foes	Treasure Acquired
Resolution: ▨ Victory ▨ Defeat ▨ .... ▨		
	Notes and Details	

Battle:	Notable Foes	Treasure Acquired
Resolution: ▨ Victory ▨ Defeat ▨ .... ▨		
	Notes and Details	

Battle:	Notable Foes	Treasure Acquired
Resolution: ▨ Victory ▨ Defeat ▨ .... ▨		
	Notes and Details	

Battle:	Notable Foes	Treasure Acquired
Resolution:		
▪ Victory		
▪ Defeat		
▪	Notes and Details	
....		
▪		
....		

Battle:	Notable Foes	Treasure Acquired
Resolution:		
▪ Victory		
▪ Defeat		
▪	Notes and Details	
....		
▪		
....		

Battle:	Notable Foes	Treasure Acquired
Resolution:		
▪ Victory		
▪ Defeat		
▪	Notes and Details	
....		
▪		
....		

ENCOUNTERS

Not every obstacle on your journey can or will be resolved at the edge of a blade. You might perform some great feat of diplomacy, explore a new and undiscovered land, meet some of the luminaries and famous warriors of your world, or encounter any number of other incredible experiences.

....

....

....

....

....

....

....

....

....

....

....

....

....

....

....

....

....

....

....

....

....

....

....

....

ADDITIONAL CAMPAIGN NOTES

....

....

....

....

....

....

....

....

....

....

....

....

....

....

....

....

....

....

....

....

....

....

....

....

....

....

....

....

....

CHARACTER THREE

Colt Cobblestone

Character Name

Remember, you can create a character any time, but it takes investment to make them yours. Spend some time thinking about your character—not only their appearance and gear, but also their backstory and their psychology. How will they react in a given situation? This is a great place to start.

CHARACTER NAME AND DESCRIPTION

To begin, you'll detail your character's name and appearance, which is what you'll reference when describing them to other players. Go big and be distinctive! The best characters are the most memorable, and bold decisions when building your look are a great place to begin. And remember: Just because you're starting your game doesn't mean your character only just popped into existence. A few nicknames, epithets, and quirks now will go a long way in the future.

CHARACTER NAME

What's in a name? Potential, for a start. Your character's name can say a lot about them, reflecting their parentage, species, nation, and calling, all while conveying brutality, beauty, or mystery.

Full Name: Colt Cobblestone

Known Aliases/Nicknames:
Gamadour De'lamont
⬆
Birth name

Titles Earned:

....

....

....

Draw your character here:

PLACE OF ORIGIN

Can folks tell where you hail from just by your gait or the cut of your hair? You might be a blank slate or wear your homeland on your sleeve like a badge. If you're looking for inspiration, consider a few of the keywords here.

Place of Origin Name:

....

Location Type:

- Plains
- Forest
- Tundra
- Coast
- ✗ City (small)
- Settlement
- Island
- Swamp
- Hills
- Mountains
- Castle/Fort
- Plane
- Planet
- Colony
- ....
- ....

Location Description
(check all that apply):

- ✗ Shimmering
- Battle-Ravaged
- Silent
- Fetid
- ✗ Noble

- Drowned
- Fae
- Calm
- Unsullied
- Stony
- Infested
- Pastoral
- Sunny
- Hardscrabble
- ✗ Enchanted
- Bustling
- Burning
- ✗ Eternal
- Vanishing
- Dead
- Broken
- Deep
- Whispering
- Forgotten
- Ruined
- Shadowy
- Windswept
- Verdant
- ....
- ....

PHYSICAL DESCRIPTION

You can convey a great deal about your character with little more than body language. Shy and slight, cloaked against the shadows? Or burly and imposing, rattling the ground you walk on? How do you make an impression without a word?

Species/Subspecies:
Rock Gnome

Height: 3'

Weight: average

Build: Short

Eye Color: blue; always wearing turquoise glowing goggles

Body Texture:

☑ Skin   ▢ Fur   ▢
☑ Hair   ▢ Feather ▢
         ▢ Scale

Coloring:

Other Defining Traits:

• Giant black gauntlets covered in magic sigils

• Long black coat that was meant for a tall elf

• Long black hair slicked up and poofy

• Reverse face hugger like mechanical device on face controlling Yogi (Pet mechanical owl)

Defining Physical Traits:

▢ Battle Scar:

▢ War Wound:

▢ Striking Feature:

▢ Magical Mutation:

▢ Curious Affectation:

▢ Mystic Special Effects:

▢ Tattoos or Scarification:

▢ Bestial Attributes:

▢ Jewelry and Piercings:

PERSONALITY

What are the day-to-day attitudes that you bring to your party and your work? Are you fun to be around? Honest and headstrong? Select all that apply.

- Pleasant
- Angry
- Morose
- ✗ Forthright
- Flamboyant
- Quiet
- Kind

- Reserved
- Outgoing
- Proud
- Selfish
- Devious
- ✗ Clever
- Witty

- Guarded
- Trusting
- Suspicious
- Sunny
- Earnest
- Withdrawn
- Lazy

- Meticulous
- ✗ Overconfident
- Modest
- Caring
- Fun
- Pessimistic
- Candid

Do you get along well with your traveling companions?

Colt gets along with everyone. It's his traveling companions whom are distrustful of Colt. But overtime he gains their trust

How do you react to strangers and potential foes?

Colt always has pockets full of odds and ends he is trying to sell. Anything to get a goll or 2. If he can make a sole he has made a successful interaction, even from a foe ~~either~~. The same could be said about picking someones pocket.

ADDITIONAL CHARACTER DESCRIPTION NOTES

Colt is an ambitious salesman. He is constantly trying to sell his magical teas that he creates via infusion. His end goal is to own a whole shop in a bustling city.

HISTORY AND BACKSTORY

Here you'll put into words the past that you've left behind as your character steps forward into the larger world of the game. Does the past haunt you? Are you followed by the remnants of a life you long to escape? Or do you miss the simplicity of the days before you stepped out onto your road? By detailing your history, you provide a map of how you'll interact with the game world now and in the future.

FAMILY BACKGROUND

Everyone comes from somewhere, even if they technically come from no one. Use this space to list your family and their status.

Father's Name: *Mr. De'lamont*

Father Is:

Living   Deceased   ☒ Unknown

....

....

....

Mother's Name: *Mrs. De'lamont*

Mother Is:

Living   Deceased   ☒ Unknown

....

....

....

Spouse/Partner Name:

....

Sibling Names and Birth Order:

....

....

....

....

....

Children/Grandchildren Names:

....

....

....

....

....

Other Family or Notable Figures' Names:

Del'lah De'lamont - Aunt

....

....

....

....

What influence did your family have on who you have become?

Colt's family treated him as the black sheep of the family he was ostracised for being

FAMILY DRAMA

A great way to build hooks and intrigue is to add some family drama that you've left behind or that still haunts you to this day. Check the list items that correspond with your character.

- A sibling fell to evil long ago. You still feel a sense of responsibility when their predation affects those you know.

- You were stolen away from a loving home as a babe and raised secretly for some evil purpose. You still wonder about your original family.

- You're next in line to the throne somewhere, which explains why assassins keep showing up.

- Your parents were replaced by something unnatural when you were small. Somehow you escaped, but you've been weary and perceptive ever since.

- You were raised by a family of another species, leaving you steeped in their culture and a little less comfortable in your own.

- You lost a great love once. You were even considering settling down. But they vanished, and that loss still drives you.

- ✗ Your family is a long lineage of a single proud work, but you never had the hands or stomach for the family business. Perhaps they still resent you for abandoning the tradition. — *couldn't do magic*

- No childhood trauma befell you or your family. You grew up peacefully and happy, content with your parents and siblings around you. Several are still among us, and you visit them for a source of strength to this day.

- ....
  ....
  ....

WEALTH STATUS

Are you living the high life, or is a rougher path for you at the moment? For some adventurers, this answer can change with ease; they find themselves rolling high after a big score, then scrabble to pay for lodging while seeking out the next job. Here, focus on your character's ideal wealth status. Where on the social strata are they the most comfortable?

- **Contented Pauper:** Scruffy, rough, and cheap even in the best of times.

- **Lean Adventurer:** Always ready to head out; it's always been about the fights instead of the scores.

- **Easy Come, Easy Goer:** You rise to the level money can buy, sleeping in barns with the same comfort as luxury suites.

- ✗ **Canny Mercantilist:** Adventure is a second business to you, and you carry wares wherever you go, offering goods and services to towns as you cross them. As such, you're usually comfortable and can expect favorable service and rates from your fellow merchant peers.

- ◉ **Savvy Grifter:** You always seem to be comfortable as long as there are enough suckers and marks in the area. The speed of your smile and wit are bested only by the speed at which you leave town.

- **Scion of Success:** Maybe your pockets are empty at the moment, but everyone knows your family has full coffers. Given your vaunted status, it would be unseemly to sleep rough.

- **High Roller:** Money is as important to you as food and water. Even in hard times, you always seem to have the little extra amenities.

- ....
  ....
  ....

HEROIC BEGINNING

There comes a time in every hero's life when they must accept that they are no longer the person they were yesterday—that they can't go back. What did your moment look like? When you stepped out the door and into a larger world, was it voluntary, or were you pushed? In the following list, you'll find a few examples of common steps that take adventurers from an old life to a new one. Choose one or make up your own.

- **Marching to Battle:** You signed up to defend your home, country, or way of life, and marched from home to war. Then you watched someone die and it changed everything.

- **Apprenticeship's End:** It was a grueling education, but even more so an abrupt end, shoved out the door with nothing but the clothes on your back and the rudimentary tools of a trade. You returned home once, but it had vanished from the face of the world.

- **Local Hero:** You weren't trained for it, but when doom befell your home, you rushed to help rather than cower and wait. Now you live for that same rush. However, you were struck by a dangerous curse.

- **Call of the Wild:** You always felt more comfortable away from the smell and noise of the crowd, and the adventurer path gave you the freedom to live outside the walls. You fell in love along the path to adventure.

- **Last Survivor:** You used to be happy, living among your kin in your hometown. But that's all gone now. Unmoored and hardened, you turned to a wandering life. Your simple journey became complicated as you mistakenly stepped into another world.

- **Lying Low:** Your last job didn't go so well. It should've been a perfect score, but the guards had changed, or you didn't see that trap. Now, shamed and wanted, you can't go home, and need to get away with your skin. You found a mystic relic early on, and your fortunes have been shaped around it.

- **An Unexpected Meeting:** You found someone or something in the shadows that offered you a bargain. A short-term job that seems to go on forever, or power at a price. You wonder if you should have said no. You lived when all signs, mystical or practical, suggest you should have died.

- **The Quest:** You set out with a single mission burning in your heart. To vanquish one foe. To retrieve one relic. Perhaps you've yet to do so, or perhaps you've completed that mission, but there are always new quests. You found the first wanted poster with your face on it a day after you walked away from home.

....

....

....

....

....

....

....

....

....

....

....

....

MOTIVATIONS

At a primal level, something calls every adventurer and hero to action. Understanding what drives your character to venture forth every day can help you steer decisions over the course of the game. Choose one of these lists and mark which of the options applies to your character.

- Looking out for the little guy
  - Used to be the little guy
  - Used to be the bully
  - Failed to defend someone in the past
  - ....
    ....
  - ....
    ....

- Seeking fame and fortune
  - Left a hardscrabble existence on hope
  - Always felt big things were coming
  - Wants the world to know your name
  - ....
    ....
  - ....
    ....

- Called to adventure by the gods
  - You've been chosen since childhood and groomed for this
  - Inspiration came in the form of a vision on the battlefield
  - You've sought out the forgiveness of the gods in atonement for a previous life of transgression
  - ....
    ....
  - ....
    ....

- Avenging a wrong
  - It's a personal vendetta the world doesn't know about
  - You seek to stop a great evil that threatens all
  - You already avenged the wrong and are seeking new purpose
  - ....
    ....
  - ....
    ....

- A perilous path to power
  - You've made a dark trade, and collection on your debt will come someday
  - The power you've attained came at a dire cost to your body and mind
  - You've left a trail of crimes behind you that you must always run from
  - ....
    ....
  - ....
    ....

- Following your hero's footsteps
  - Your hero was the hero of your people—many follow in their footsteps; few succeed
  - Someone saved your life once, and you are compelled not to waste that gift
  - Your hero may have fallen but you have learned from their example all the same
  - ....
    ....
  - ....
    ....

Following a trusted friend

- Childhood friends for life
- Your mentor vanished, leaving only cryptic clues
- The spirit of a fallen compatriot spurs you onward

Displaced from home

- You still hold a grudge against those who destroyed your old life
- You were separated from your home by disaster
- You earned your banishment and bear that shame

Trained for combat but the war is over

- Selling your sword arm beats life on the farm
- The war may be over but you haven't forgotten or forgiven
- You developed a taste for conflict and seek it out to this day

GEAR AND OTHER ITEMS OF INTEREST

Whether you're considering the basics, like fifty feet of silken rope plus flint and tinder, or the truly unique, like the enchanted eye of the last green dragon or a hot-rodded custom starfighter, the trappings you carry around convey a story, and that story can be as simple or as complex as your own history. In this section, list your weapons, equipment, and miscellaneous items you possess or have decided to bring with you.

GEAR

Consider the general state of your belongings. Are you a fastidious adventurer who keeps each item organized, clean, and in good working order? Do you let things fall into messy disrepair, counting on good fortune and jerry-rigging to keep your tools useful?

Weapons

Did you begin your adventuring career with the only weapon you'll ever need? A trusted heirloom or sainted magic relic that will see you through all hardship? Or do you replace weapons with the ease of breathing, always seeking the next upgrade? Here, you'll detail your favorite weapons and your relationship to them.

Secondary Weapons

Even the most stringent devotee to the arts of the blade may carry more than one weapon, just in case. Here, list any other weapons you carry or have gathered on the journey.

Weapon (circle one)	Name	Model	Stats and Bonuses	History
primary secondary				
primary secondary				
primary secondary				
primary secondary				
primary secondary				
primary secondary				
primary secondary				

Gear Goals

It's not often that you get the chance to start the game with everything you want, and it doesn't matter if your target is something you need for quest purposes or just a wizard staff you happen to think looks particularly good with your current hat: A large part of adventuring is heading out to get what you want. So, think about just that: what you want. This space can serve as a reminder, a wish list for an interested game master (GM), or just a set of goals to put out in the world.

Item	Description	Probable Location

Gear Relationship

- Nothing but the weapons and the clothes on your back
- Packed for emergencies
- Packed for comfort
- Prepared for everything
- Compulsive collector
- ....

Storage Style

- Organized
- Untidy
- Stored in pouches and straps
- Carried by underlings
- Stored in otherspace
- Kept in the saddlebags
- Hidden on yourself
- ....

Gear Appearance

- Neglected
- Piecemeal
- Rusted
- Stolen
- Handcrafted
- Heirloom
- Store-bought
- Polished
- Customized
- Mystical
- ....

TREASURED BELONGINGS

There's always room on your character sheet for the basics, but not every piece of equipment you're carrying is basic. Here you can list the things that have real significance and importance, whether that be to the campaign at large or just to you. Whether it's as simple as a locket with a photo or as epic as the only rock left of your demolished home world, certain items are just more important.

Item:

Description	Origin	
	▨ Birthright	▨ Crafted
	▨ Claimed	▨ Reward
	▨ Discovered	▨ Other:
	▨ Stole	....
	▨ Purchased	....

Item:

Description	Origin	
	▨ Birthright	▨ Crafted
	▨ Claimed	▨ Reward
	▨ Discovered	▨ Other:
	▨ Stole	....
	▨ Purchased	....

Item:

Description	Origin	
	▨ Birthright	▨ Crafted
	▨ Claimed	▨ Reward
	▨ Discovered	▨ Other:
	▨ Stole	....
	▨ Purchased	....

Item:	
Description	**Origin**
	▧ Birthright ▧ Crafted ▧ Claimed ▧ Reward ▧ Discovered ▧ Other: ▧ Stole .... ▧ Purchased ....

Item:	
Description	**Origin**
	▧ Birthright ▧ Crafted ▧ Claimed ▧ Reward ▧ Discovered ▧ Other: ▧ Stole .... ▧ Purchased ....

Item:	
Description	**Origin**
	▧ Birthright ▧ Crafted ▧ Claimed ▧ Reward ▧ Discovered ▧ Other: ▧ Stole .... ▧ Purchased ....

Item:	
Description	**Origin**
	▧ Birthright ▧ Crafted ▧ Claimed ▧ Reward ▧ Discovered ▧ Other: ▧ Stole .... ▧ Purchased ....

PROPERTY

Have you come into possession of something large enough that it requires titles and deeds, as well as maintenance or even a constant staff for upkeep? Perhaps a secret lair, an office for your paranormal investigations, a starcruiser, or a beat-up car that'll get from point A to B if you baby it enough? When you take ownership of conveyance or property, record it here.

Property Type:

- ▦ Vehicle/Steed   ▦ Country
- ▦ Home   ▦ Planet
- ▦ Business   ▦ ....
- ▦ Town/City   ▦ ....
- ▦ Kingdom

Property Location: ....
....
....

Description: ....
....
....

Condition: ....
....
....

Property Type:

- ▦ Vehicle/Steed   ▦ Country
- ▦ Home   ▦ Planet
- ▦ Business   ▦ ....
- ▦ Town/City   ▦ ....
- ▦ Kingdom

Property Location: ....
....
....

Description: ....
....
....

Condition: ....
....
....

ADDITIONAL ITEM NOTES

....
....
....
....
....
....
....
....
....
....
....
....
....
....
....
....
....
....
....
....
....
....
....
....
....
....
....
....
....
....
....
....
....
....
....
....
....

ABILITIES OF NOTE

As you progress through your game world, you'll become ever more competent at your chosen field(s). Warriors become stronger and more tactically capable; casters add an ever-increasing array of arcane and divine tricks to their arsenal; negotiators become increasingly versed in matters of diplomacy and discussion; and so on. Here you'll record a list of your most efficacious and incredible abilities, along with notes describing how you personalize them to make them truly yours.

SIGNATURE ABILITIES

A perfect blade swing that can cut through the air itself. A softly spoken word that can divert the course of an empire. A granted miracle that calls down heaven itself to cast away the dead. Many characters will come to be known for such incredible feats, and those signature techniques they have will bear their names into legend.

Skill Name:	▨ Physical ▨ Divine ▨ Technological ▨ Mental ▨ Social ▨ .... ▨ Magical ▨ Artifact ▨		
Skill Effect:	Personal Upgrades:		Element Change:
Increased Range:	Increased Power:		Visual Special Effects:
Power Source (check one):			
▨ Innate:	▨ Taught:		▨ Bestowed:
▨ Upgrade:	▨ Other:		▨ Other:

Skill Name:	▨ Physical	▨ Divine	▨ Technological
	▨ Mental	▨ Social	▨ ....
	▨ Magical	▨ Artifact	▨ ....

Skill Effect:	Personal Upgrades:	Element Change:
Increased Range:	Increased Power:	Visual Special Effects:

Power Source (check one):

▨ Innate:	▨ Taught:	▨ Bestowed:
▨ Upgrade:	▨ Other:	▨ Other:

Skill Name:	▨ Physical	▨ Divine	▨ Technological
	▨ Mental	▨ Social	▨ ....
	▨ Magical	▨ Artifact	▨ ....

Skill Effect:	Personal Upgrades:	Element Change:
Increased Range:	Increased Power:	Visual Special Effects:

Power Source (check one):

▨ Innate:	▨ Taught:	▨ Bestowed:
▨ Upgrade:	▨ Other:	▨ Other:

COMPLETE TOOL KIT

Adventurers may make their legacy on the flash and drama of their most powerful tools, but they survive long enough to earn that legacy through growth and maintenance of a suite of survival, combat, and social tools ranging from beginners' survival tools to expert techniques.

Skill Name:	Skill Name:	Skill Name:	Skill Name:	Skill Name:
Type:	Type:	Type:	Type:	Type:
▪ Technique ▪ Spell ▪ Power ▪ .... ▪	▪ Technique ▪ Spell ▪ Power ▪ .... ▪	▪ Technique ▪ Spell ▪ Power ▪ .... ▪	▪ Technique ▪ Spell ▪ Power ▪ .... ▪	▪ Technique ▪ Spell ▪ Power ▪ .... ▪ ....
Description	**Description**	**Description**	**Description**	**Description**
Stats and Bonuses	**Stats and Bonuses**	**Stats and Bonuses**	**Stats and Bonuses**	**Stats and Bonuses**
Special Effects	**Special Effects**	**Special Effects**	**Special Effects**	**Special Effects**

NON-PLAYER CHARACTERS

Nobody goes through life without making some connections with the people around them, and your character should be no different. Whether it's someone you consider as close to you as a member of your own family, or a simple shop owner that you know has the best prices in town, these are the folks around you that mean the most.

CHARACTER

Character Name: ....

Character Type:

- ▣ Government Official/Politician
- ▣ Business Owner
- ▣ Family Member
- ▣ Non-Party Adventurer
- ▣ Faction or Gang Leader
- ▣ Guard/Soldier
- ▣ Refugee/Person in Need
- ▣ Old Friend
- ▣ Teacher/Expert
- ▣ Monster
- ▣ Courier
- ▣ Child/Youth
- ▣ Extraplanar/Extraplanetary Visitor
- ▣ ....
- ▣ ....

Relationship:

- ▣ Friendly
- ▣ Transactional
- ▣ Competitive
- ▣ Adversarial
- ▣ Violent
- ▣ ....
- ▣ ....

Physical Description: ....
....
....
....
....
....

Character Personality:

- ▣ Shifty. Paranoid. Always looking around.
- ▣ Boisterous. Welcoming. Calls you "friend."
- ▣ Serious. All business. No sense of humor.
- ▣ Friendly. Gentle. Likes being helpful.
- ▣ Cowardly. Whiny. Hates being called on.
- ▣ Gruff. Grumpy. Grudgingly does business with you.
- ▣ Greedy. Slick. In it for the profit.
- ▣ Flirty. Charming. Makes you feel special.
- ▣ Bombastic. Dramatic. All eyes on them.
- ▣ ....
- ▣ ....
- ▣ ....
- ▣ ....

What They Can Do for You:

- ▣ Has your back in any adventure
- ▣ Provides mentorship and guidance
- ▣ Boosts your ego with praise and admiration
- ▣ Always has the latest gossip
- ▣ Buys or sells contraband and rare items
- ▣ Knows when big crimes are happening
- ▣ Can introduce you to people you need
- ▣ Sells discounted goods
- ▣ Owes you an undetermined favor
- ▣ Gives you a place to crash and lie low
- ▣ Can get you the information you need
- ▣ Gets anything/anyone where it needs to go
- ▣ ....
- ▣ ....
- ▣ ....
- ▣ ....

OTHER CHARACTERS OF NOTE

There are plenty of people in the world that you hear of but don't directly interact with. The name of the local governor that might come in handy lately. The employer who sent you on your latest job. Even the bartender at your favorite hangout might be worth remembering and coming back to. Feel free to jot down anyone that feels important to remember.

ADDITIONAL NPC NOTES

CAMPAIGN NOTES

Herein lies your opportunity to record the great (and the infamous) deeds of your character and their journey. As they grow in power and glory, you'll be able to document each slain foe and each well-met hero on your road, and reflect back on the early days of your starting career. Additionally, it never hurts to keep a record, in case you forget an important name or person who will assuredly crop up later.

PARTY MEMBERS

It's rare that you'll venture forth to adventure alone. Who watches your back? Do you trust them implicitly or do you keep one eye open? You can list the important events and interactions here, or note down the small details to call up again when role-playing in the future.

IMPORTANT EVENTS

How have you made your mark on the world? When the lyricists compose your ode, what stories will they lean on, and what dark paths and mistakes will they carefully elide? Be sure to mention the people you met along the way too, since you never know when they'll turn up again.

BATTLES

There's certainly no reason you can't use this section as a hunting journal or scoreboard, simply listing the types and vitals of every orc or space bug you dispatch. But you might also want to focus on the epic events, the villains that brought you to the edge of doom, or the moments of good fortune or tactical brilliance that make the best boastful brags.

Battle:	Notable Foes	Treasure Acquired
Resolution:		
▢ Victory		
▢ Defeat	Notes and Details	
▢		
....		
▢		
....		

Battle:	Notable Foes	Treasure Acquired
Resolution:		
▢ Victory		
▢ Defeat	Notes and Details	
▢		
....		
▢		
....		

Battle:	Notable Foes	Treasure Acquired
Resolution:		
▢ Victory		
▢ Defeat	Notes and Details	
▢		
....		
▢		
....		

Battle:	Notable Foes	Treasure Acquired
Resolution:		
▨ Victory		
▨ Defeat	**Notes and Details**	
▨		
....		
▨		
....		

Battle:	Notable Foes	Treasure Acquired
Resolution:		
▨ Victory		
▨ Defeat	**Notes and Details**	
▨		
....		
▨		
....		

Battle:	Notable Foes	Treasure Acquired
Resolution:		
▨ Victory		
▨ Defeat	**Notes and Details**	
▨		
....		
▨		
....		

ENCOUNTERS

Not every obstacle on your journey can or will be resolved at the edge of a blade. You might perform some great feat of diplomacy, explore a new and undiscovered land, meet some of the luminaries and famous warriors of your world, or encounter any number of other incredible experiences.

....

....

....

....

....

....

....

....

....

....

....

....

....

....

....

....

....

....

....

....

....

....

....

....

....

ADDITIONAL CAMPAIGN NOTES

....

....

....

....

....

....

....

....

....

....

....

....

....

....

....

....

....

....

....

....

....

....

....

....

....

....

....

....

....

....

....

....

....

CHARACTER FOUR

Character Name

Remember, you can create a character any time, but it takes investment to make them yours. Spend some time thinking about your character—not only their appearance and gear, but also their backstory and their psychology. How will they react in a given situation? This is a great place to start.

CHARACTER NAME AND DESCRIPTION

To begin, you'll detail your character's name and appearance, which is what you'll reference when describing them to other players. Go big and be distinctive! The best characters are the most memorable, and bold decisions when building your look are a great place to begin. And remember: Just because you're starting your game doesn't mean your character only just popped into existence. A few nicknames, epithets, and quirks now will go a long way in the future.

CHARACTER NAME

What's in a name? Potential, for a start. Your character's name can say a lot about them, reflecting their parentage, species, nation, and calling, all while conveying brutality, beauty, or mystery.

Full Name: ....

Known Aliases/Nicknames:

....

....

....

Titles Earned:

....

....

....

Draw your character here:

PLACE OF ORIGIN

Can folks tell where you hail from just by your gait or the cut of your hair? You might be a blank slate or wear your homeland on your sleeve like a badge. If you're looking for inspiration, consider a few of the keywords here.

Place of Origin Name:

....

Location Type:

- Plains
- Forest
- Tundra
- Coast
- City
- Settlement
- Island
- Swamp
- Hills
- Mountains
- Castle/Fort
- Plane
- Planet
- Colony
- ....
- ....

Location Description (check all that apply):

- Shimmering
- Battle-Ravaged
- Silent
- Fetid
- Noble
- Drowned
- Fae
- Calm
- Unsullied
- Stony
- Infested
- Pastoral
- Sunny
- Hardscrabble
- Enchanted
- Bustling
- Burning
- Eternal
- Vanishing
- Dead
- Broken
- Deep
- Whispering
- Forgotten
- Ruined
- Shadowy
- Windswept
- Verdant
- ....
- ....

PHYSICAL DESCRIPTION

You can convey a great deal about your character with little more than body language. Shy and slight, cloaked against the shadows? Or burly and imposing, rattling the ground you walk on? How do you make an impression without a word?

Species/Subspecies:

....

Height: ....

Weight: ....

Build: ....

Eye Color: ....

Body Texture:

- ▨ Skin   ▨ Fur   ▨ ....
- ▨ Hair   ▨ Feather   ▨ ....
-             ▨ Scale

Coloring:

....

....

Other Defining Traits:

....

....

....

....

....

....

....

....

....

....

....

Defining Physical Traits:

▨ Battle Scar:

....

....

....

▨ War Wound:

....

....

....

▨ Striking Feature:

....

....

....

▨ Magical Mutation:

....

....

....

▨ Curious Affectation:

....

....

....

▨ Mystic Special Effects:

....

....

....

▨ Tattoos or Scarification:

....

....

....

▨ Bestial Attributes:

....

....

....

▨ Jewelry and Piercings:

....

....

....

PERSONALITY

What are the day-to-day attitudes that you bring to your party and your work? Are you fun to be around? Honest and headstrong? Select all that apply.

- Pleasant
- Angry
- Morose
- Forthright
- Flamboyant
- Quiet
- Kind

- Reserved
- Outgoing
- Proud
- Selfish
- Devious
- Clever
- Witty

- Guarded
- Trusting
- Suspicious
- Sunny
- Earnest
- Withdrawn
- Lazy

- Meticulous
- Overconfident
- Modest
- Caring
- Fun
- Pessimistic
- Candid

Do you get along well with your traveling companions?

....
....
....
....
....
....
....
....

How do you react to strangers and potential foes?

....
....
....
....
....
....
....
....

ADDITIONAL CHARACTER DESCRIPTION NOTES

....
....
....
....
....
....
....
....
....
....

HISTORY AND BACKSTORY

Here you'll put into words the past that you've left behind as your character steps forward into the larger world of the game. Does the past haunt you? Are you followed by the remnants of a life you long to escape? Or do you miss the simplicity of the days before you stepped out onto your road? By detailing your history, you provide a map of how you'll interact with the game world now and in the future.

FAMILY BACKGROUND

Everyone comes from somewhere, even if they technically come from no one. Use this space to list your family and their status.

Father's Name: ....

Father Is:

- ▨ Living   ▨ Deceased   ▨ Unknown

- ▨ ....

- ▨ ....

Mother's Name: ....

Mother Is:

- ▨ Living   ▨ Deceased   ▨ Unknown

- ▨ ....

- ▨ ....

Spouse/Partner Name:

....

Sibling Names and Birth Order:

....

....

....

....

Children/Grandchildren Names:

....

....

....

....

....

....

Other Family or Notable Figures' Names:

....

....

....

....

What influence did your family have on who you have become?

....

....

....

....

....

....

....

....

FAMILY DRAMA

A great way to build hooks and intrigue is to add some family drama that you've left behind or that still haunts you to this day. Check the list items that correspond with your character.

- A sibling fell to evil long ago. You still feel a sense of responsibility when their predation affects those you know.

- You were stolen away from a loving home as a babe and raised secretly for some evil purpose. You still wonder about your original family.

- You're next in line to the throne somewhere, which explains why assassins keep showing up.

- Your parents were replaced by something unnatural when you were small. Somehow you escaped, but you've been weary and perceptive ever since.

- You were raised by a family of another species, leaving you steeped in their culture and a little less comfortable in your own.

- You lost a great love once. You were even considering settling down. But they vanished, and that loss still drives you.

- Your family is a long lineage of a single proud work, but you never had the hands or stomach for the family business. Perhaps they still resent you for abandoning the tradition.

- No childhood trauma befell you or your family. You grew up peacefully and happy, content with your parents and siblings around you. Several are still among us, and you visit them for a source of strength to this day.

- ....

- ....

WEALTH STATUS

Are you living the high life, or is a rougher path for you at the moment? For some adventurers, this answer can change with ease; they find themselves rolling high after a big score, then scrabble to pay for lodging while seeking out the next job. Here, focus on your character's ideal wealth status. Where on the social strata are they the most comfortable?

- **Contented Pauper:** Scruffy, rough, and cheap even in the best of times.

- **Lean Adventurer:** Always ready to head out; it's always been about the fights instead of the scores.

- **Easy Come, Easy Goer:** You rise to the level money can buy, sleeping in barns with the same comfort as luxury suites.

- **Canny Mercantilist:** Adventure is a second business to you, and you carry wares wherever you go, offering goods and services to towns as you cross them. As such, you're usually comfortable and can expect favorable service and rates from your fellow merchant peers.

- **Savvy Grifter:** You always seem to be comfortable as long as there are enough suckers and marks in the area. The speed of your smile and wit are bested only by the speed at which you leave town.

- **Scion of Success:** Maybe your pockets are empty at the moment, but everyone knows your family has full coffers. Given your vaunted status, it would be unseemly to sleep rough.

- **High Roller:** Money is as important to you as food and water. Even in hard times, you always seem to have the little extra amenities.

- ....

- ....

HEROIC BEGINNING

There comes a time in every hero's life when they must accept that they are no longer the person they were yesterday—that they can't go back. What did your moment look like? When you stepped out the door and into a larger world, was it voluntary, or were you pushed? In the following list, you'll find a few examples of common steps that take adventurers from an old life to a new one. Choose one or make up your own.

- **Marching to Battle:** You signed up to defend your home, country, or way of life, and marched from home to war. Then you watched someone die and it changed everything.

- **Apprenticeship's End:** It was a grueling education, but even more so an abrupt end, shoved out the door with nothing but the clothes on your back and the rudimentary tools of a trade. You returned home once, but it had vanished from the face of the world.

- **Local Hero:** You weren't trained for it, but when doom befell your home, you rushed to help rather than cower and wait. Now you live for that same rush. However, you were struck by a dangerous curse.

- **Call of the Wild:** You always felt more comfortable away from the smell and noise of the crowd, and the adventurer path gave you the freedom to live outside the walls. You fell in love along the path to adventure.

- **Last Survivor:** You used to be happy, living among your kin in your hometown. But that's all gone now. Unmoored and hardened, you turned to a wandering life. Your simple journey became complicated as you mistakenly stepped into another world.

- **Lying Low:** Your last job didn't go so well. It should've been a perfect score, but the guards had changed, or you didn't see that trap. Now, shamed and wanted, you can't go home, and need to get away with your skin. You found a mystic relic early on, and your fortunes have been shaped around it.

- **An Unexpected Meeting:** You found someone or something in the shadows that offered you a bargain. A short-term job that seems to go on forever, or power at a price. You wonder if you should have said no. You lived when all signs, mystical or practical, suggest you should have died.

- **The Quest:** You set out with a single mission burning in your heart. To vanquish one foe. To retrieve one relic. Perhaps you've yet to do so, or perhaps you've completed that mission, but there are always new quests. You found the first wanted poster with your face on it a day after you walked away from home.

....
....
....
....
....
....
....
....
....
....
....
....

MOTIVATIONS

At a primal level, something calls every adventurer and hero to action. Understanding what drives your character to venture forth every day can help you steer decisions over the course of the game. Choose one of these lists and mark which of the options applies to your character.

Looking out for the little guy

- Used to be the little guy
- Used to be the bully
- Failed to defend someone in the past
- ....
- ....
- ....
- ....

Seeking fame and fortune

- Left a hardscrabble existence on hope
- Always felt big things were coming
- Wants the world to know your name
- ....
- ....
- ....
- ....

Called to adventure by the gods

- You've been chosen since childhood and groomed for this
- Inspiration came in the form of a vision on the battlefield
- You've sought out the forgiveness of the gods in atonement for a previous life of transgression
- ....
- ....
- ....
- ....

Avenging a wrong

- It's a personal vendetta the world doesn't know about
- You seek to stop a great evil that threatens all
- You already avenged the wrong and are seeking new purpose
- ....
- ....
- ....
- ....

A perilous path to power

- You've made a dark trade, and collection on your debt will come someday
- The power you've attained came at a dire cost to your body and mind
- You've left a trail of crimes behind you that you must always run from
- ....
- ....
- ....
- ....

Following your hero's footsteps

- Your hero was the hero of your people—many follow in their footsteps; few succeed
- Someone saved your life once, and you are compelled not to waste that gift
- Your hero may have fallen but you have learned from their example all the same
- ....
- ....
- ....
- ....

Following a trusted friend

- Childhood friends for life
- Your mentor vanished, leaving only cryptic clues
- The spirit of a fallen compatriot spurs you onward
- ....
  ....
- ....
  ....

Displaced from home

- You still hold a grudge against those who destroyed your old life
- You were separated from your home by disaster
- You earned your banishment and bear that shame
- ....
  ....
- ....
  ....

Trained for combat but the war is over

- Selling your sword arm beats life on the farm
- The war may be over but you haven't forgotten or forgiven
- You developed a taste for conflict and seek it out to this day
- ....
  ....
- ....
  ....

GEAR AND OTHER ITEMS OF INTEREST

Whether you're considering the basics, like fifty feet of silken rope plus flint and tinder, or the truly unique, like the enchanted eye of the last green dragon or a hot-rodded custom star-fighter, the trappings you carry around convey a story, and that story can be as simple or as complex as your own history. In this section, list your weapons, equipment, and miscellaneous items you possess or have decided to bring with you.

GEAR

Consider the general state of your belongings. Are you a fastidious adventurer who keeps each item organized, clean, and in good working order? Do you let things fall into messy disrepair, counting on good fortune and jerry-rigging to keep your tools useful?

Weapons

Did you begin your adventuring career with the only weapon you'll ever need? A trusted heirloom or sainted magic relic that will see you through all hardship? Or do you replace weapons with the ease of breathing, always seeking the next upgrade? Here, you'll detail your favorite weapons and your relationship to them.

Secondary Weapons

Even the most stringent devotee to the arts of the blade may carry more than one weapon, just in case. Here, list any other weapons you carry or have gathered on the journey.

Weapon (circle one)	Name	Model	Stats and Bonuses	History
primary secondary				
primary secondary				
primary secondary				
primary secondary				
primary secondary				
primary secondary				
primary secondary				

Gear Goals

It's not often that you get the chance to start the game with everything you want, and it doesn't matter if your target is something you need for quest purposes or just a wizard staff you happen to think looks particularly good with your current hat: A large part of adventuring is heading out to get what you want. So, think about just that: what you want. This space can serve as a reminder, a wish list for an interested game master (GM), or just a set of goals to put out in the world.

Item	Description	Probable Location

Gear Relationship

- Nothing but the weapons and the clothes on your back
- Packed for emergencies
- Packed for comfort
- Prepared for everything
- Compulsive collector
- ....

Storage Style

- Organized
- Untidy
- Stored in pouches and straps
- Carried by underlings
- Stored in otherspace
- Kept in the saddlebags
- Hidden on yourself
- ....

Gear Appearance

- Neglected
- Piecemeal
- Rusted
- Stolen
- Handcrafted
- Heirloom
- Store-bought
- Polished
- Customized
- Mystical
- ....

TREASURED BELONGINGS

There's always room on your character sheet for the basics, but not every piece of equipment you're carrying is basic. Here you can list the things that have real significance and importance, whether that be to the campaign at large or just to you. Whether it's as simple as a locket with a photo or as epic as the only rock left of your demolished home world, certain items are just more important.

Item:	
Description	Origin
	▨ Birthright ▨ Crafted ▨ Claimed ▨ Reward ▨ Discovered ▨ Other: ▨ Stole .... ▨ Purchased ....

Item:	
Description	Origin
	▨ Birthright ▨ Crafted ▨ Claimed ▨ Reward ▨ Discovered ▨ Other: ▨ Stole .... ▨ Purchased ....

Item:	
Description	Origin
	▨ Birthright ▨ Crafted ▨ Claimed ▨ Reward ▨ Discovered ▨ Other: ▨ Stole .... ▨ Purchased ....

Item:	
Description	**Origin**
	▨ Birthright ▨ Crafted ▨ Claimed ▨ Reward ▨ Discovered ▨ Other: ▨ Stole .... ▨ Purchased ....

Item:	
Description	**Origin**
	▨ Birthright ▨ Crafted ▨ Claimed ▨ Reward ▨ Discovered ▨ Other: ▨ Stole .... ▨ Purchased ....

Item:	
Description	**Origin**
	▨ Birthright ▨ Crafted ▨ Claimed ▨ Reward ▨ Discovered ▨ Other: ▨ Stole .... ▨ Purchased ....

Item:	
Description	**Origin**
	▨ Birthright ▨ Crafted ▨ Claimed ▨ Reward ▨ Discovered ▨ Other: ▨ Stole .... ▨ Purchased ....

PROPERTY

Have you come into possession of something large enough that it requires titles and deeds, as well as maintenance or even a constant staff for upkeep? Perhaps a secret lair, an office for your paranormal investigations, a starcruiser, or a beat-up car that'll get from point A to B if you baby it enough? When you take ownership of conveyance or property, record it here.

Property Type:

- ▨ Vehicle/Steed   ▨ Country
- ▨ Home   ▨ Planet
- ▨ Business   ▨ ....
- ▨ Town/City   ▨ ....
- ▨ Kingdom

Property Location: ....
....
....

Description: ....
....
....

Condition: ....
....
....

Property Type:

- ▨ Vehicle/Steed   ▨ Country
- ▨ Home   ▨ Planet
- ▨ Business   ▨ ....
- ▨ Town/City   ▨ ....
- ▨ Kingdom

Property Location: ....
....
....

Description: ....
....
....

Condition: ....
....
....

ADDITIONAL ITEM NOTES

....
....
....
....
....
....
....
....
....
....
....
....
....
....
....
....
....
....
....
....
....
....
....
....
....
....
....
....
....
....
....
....
....
....
....
....
....
....

ABILITIES OF NOTE

As you progress through your game world, you'll become ever more competent at your chosen field(s). Warriors become stronger and more tactically capable; casters add an ever-increasing array of arcane and divine tricks to their arsenal; negotiators become increasingly versed in matters of diplomacy and discussion; and so on. Here you'll record a list of your most efficacious and incredible abilities, along with notes describing how you personalize them to make them truly yours.

SIGNATURE ABILITIES

A perfect blade swing that can cut through the air itself. A softly spoken word that can divert the course of an empire. A granted miracle that calls down heaven itself to cast away the dead. Many characters will come to be known for such incredible feats, and those signature techniques they have will bear their names into legend.

Skill Name:	▨ Physical ▨ Divine ▨ Technological ▨ Mental ▨ Social ▨ .... ▨ Magical ▨ Artifact ▨	
Skill Effect:	Personal Upgrades:	Element Change:
Increased Range:	Increased Power:	Visual Special Effects:
Power Source (check one):		
▨ Innate:	▨ Taught:	▨ Bestowed:
▨ Upgrade:	▨ Other:	▨ Other:

Skill Name:	☒ Physical ☒ Divine ☒ Technological
	☒ Mental ☒ Social ☒ ....
	☒ Magical ☒ Artifact ☒ ....

Skill Effect:	Personal Upgrades:	Element Change:

Increased Range:	Increased Power:	Visual Special Effects:

Power Source (check one):

☒ Innate:	☒ Taught:	☒ Bestowed:
☒ Upgrade:	☒ Other:	☒ Other:

Skill Name:	☒ Physical ☒ Divine ☒ Technological
	☒ Mental ☒ Social ☒ ....
	☒ Magical ☒ Artifact ☒ ....

Skill Effect:	Personal Upgrades:	Element Change:

Increased Range:	Increased Power:	Visual Special Effects:

Power Source (check one):

☒ Innate:	☒ Taught:	☒ Bestowed:
☒ Upgrade:	☒ Other:	☒ Other:

COMPLETE TOOL KIT

Adventurers may make their legacy on the flash and drama of their most powerful tools, but they survive long enough to earn that legacy through growth and maintenance of a suite of survival, combat, and social tools ranging from beginners' survival tools to expert techniques.

Skill Name:	Skill Name:	Skill Name:	Skill Name:	Skill Name:
....	....	....	....	....
Type:	Type:	Type:	Type:	Type:
▪ Technique	▪ Technique	▪ Technique	▪ Technique	▪ Technique
▪ Spell	▪ Spell	▪ Spell	▪ Spell	▪ Spell
▪ Power	▪ Power	▪ Power	▪ Power	▪ Power
▪	▪	▪	▪	▪ ....
▪	▪	▪	▪	▪ ....
Description	**Description**	**Description**	**Description**	**Description**
Stats and Bonuses	**Stats and Bonuses**	**Stats and Bonuses**	**Stats and Bonuses**	**Stats and Bonuses**
Special Effects	**Special Effects**	**Special Effects**	**Special Effects**	**Special Effects**

NON-PLAYER CHARACTERS

Nobody goes through life without making some connections with the people around them, and your character should be no different. Whether it's someone you consider as close to you as a member of your own family, or a simple shop owner that you know has the best prices in town, these are the folks around you that mean the most.

CHARACTER

Character Name: ....

Character Type:

- ▦ Government Official/Politician
- ▦ Business Owner
- ▦ Family Member
- ▦ Non-Party Adventurer
- ▦ Faction or Gang Leader
- ▦ Guard/Soldier
- ▦ Refugee/Person in Need
- ▦ Old Friend
- ▦ Teacher/Expert
- ▦ Monster
- ▦ Courier
- ▦ Child/Youth
- ▦ Extraplanar/Extraplanetary Visitor
- ▦ ....
- ▦ ....

Relationship:

- ▦ Friendly
- ▦ Transactional
- ▦ Competitive
- ▦ Adversarial
- ▦ Violent
- ▦ ....
- ▦ ....

Physical Description: ....
....
....
....
....
....

Character Personality:

- ▦ Shifty. Paranoid. Always looking around.
- ▦ Boisterous. Welcoming. Calls you "friend."
- ▦ Serious. All business. No sense of humor.
- ▦ Friendly. Gentle. Likes being helpful.
- ▦ Cowardly. Whiny. Hates being called on.
- ▦ Gruff. Grumpy. Grudgingly does business with you.
- ▦ Greedy. Slick. In it for the profit.
- ▦ Flirty. Charming. Makes you feel special.
- ▦ Bombastic. Dramatic. All eyes on them.
- ▦ ....
- ▦ ....
- ▦ ....
- ▦ ....

What They Can Do for You:

- ▦ Has your back in any adventure
- ▦ Provides mentorship and guidance
- ▦ Boosts your ego with praise and admiration
- ▦ Always has the latest gossip
- ▦ Buys or sells contraband and rare items
- ▦ Knows when big crimes are happening
- ▦ Can introduce you to people you need
- ▦ Sells discounted goods
- ▦ Owes you an undetermined favor
- ▦ Gives you a place to crash and lie low
- ▦ Can get you the information you need
- ▦ Gets anything/anyone where it needs to go
- ▦ ....
- ▦ ....
- ▦ ....

OTHER CHARACTERS OF NOTE

There are plenty of people in the world that you hear of but don't directly interact with. The name of the local governor that might come in handy lately. The employer who sent you on your latest job. Even the bartender at your favorite hangout might be worth remembering and coming back to. Feel free to jot down anyone that feels important to remember.

ADDITIONAL NPC NOTES

CAMPAIGN NOTES

Herein lies your opportunity to record the great (and the infamous) deeds of your character and their journey. As they grow in power and glory, you'll be able to document each slain foe and each well-met hero on your road, and reflect back on the early days of your starting career. Additionally, it never hurts to keep a record, in case you forget an important name or person who will assuredly crop up later.

PARTY MEMBERS

It's rare that you'll venture forth to adventure alone. Who watches your back? Do you trust them implicitly or do you keep one eye open? You can list the important events and interactions here, or note down the small details to call up again when role-playing in the future.

....
....
....
....
....
....
....
....
....
....
....
....
....
....
....
....
....
....
....
....
....

IMPORTANT EVENTS

How have you made your mark on the world? When the lyricists compose your ode, what stories will they lean on, and what dark paths and mistakes will they carefully elide? Be sure to mention the people you met along the way too, since you never know when they'll turn up again.

....
....
....
....
....
....
....
....
....
....
....
....
....
....
....
....
....
....
....
....
....

BATTLES

There's certainly no reason you can't use this section as a hunting journal or scoreboard, simply listing the types and vitals of every orc or space bug you dispatch. But you might also want to focus on the epic events, the villains that brought you to the edge of doom, or the moments of good fortune or tactical brilliance that make the best boastful brags.

Battle:	Notable Foes	Treasure Acquired
Resolution: ▢ Victory ▢ Defeat ▢ .... ▢		
	Notes and Details	

Battle:	Notable Foes	Treasure Acquired
Resolution: ▢ Victory ▢ Defeat ▢ .... ▢		
	Notes and Details	

Battle:	Notable Foes	Treasure Acquired
Resolution: ▢ Victory ▢ Defeat ▢ .... ▢		
	Notes and Details	

Battle:	Notable Foes	Treasure Acquired
Resolution: ▓ Victory ▓ Defeat ▓ .... ▓		
	Notes and Details	

Battle:	Notable Foes	Treasure Acquired
Resolution: ▓ Victory ▓ Defeat ▓ .... ▓		
	Notes and Details	

Battle:	Notable Foes	Treasure Acquired
Resolution: ▓ Victory ▓ Defeat ▓ .... ▓		
	Notes and Details	

ENCOUNTERS

Not every obstacle on your journey can or will be resolved at the edge of a blade. You might perform some great feat of diplomacy, explore a new and undiscovered land, meet some of the luminaries and famous warriors of your world, or encounter any number of other incredible experiences.

....
....
....
....
....
....
....
....
....
....
....
....
....
....
....
....
....
....
....
....
....
....
....
....
....
....

ADDITIONAL CAMPAIGN NOTES

....
....
....
....
....
....
....
....
....
....
....
....
....
....
....
....
....
....
....
....
....
....
....
....
....
....
....
....
....

CHARACTER FIVE

Character Name

Remember, you can create a character any time, but it takes investment to make them yours. Spend some time thinking about your character—not only their appearance and gear, but also their backstory and their psychology. How will they react in a given situation? This is a great place to start.

CHARACTER NAME AND DESCRIPTION

To begin, you'll detail your character's name and appearance, which is what you'll reference when describing them to other players. Go big and be distinctive! The best characters are the most memorable, and bold decisions when building your look are a great place to begin. And remember: Just because you're starting your game doesn't mean your character only just popped into existence. A few nicknames, epithets, and quirks now will go a long way in the future.

CHARACTER NAME

What's in a name? Potential, for a start. Your character's name can say a lot about them, reflecting their parentage, species, nation, and calling, all while conveying brutality, beauty, or mystery.

Full Name: ....

Known Aliases/Nicknames:

....

....

....

Titles Earned:

....

....

....

Draw your character here:

PLACE OF ORIGIN

Can folks tell where you hail from just by your gait or the cut of your hair? You might be a blank slate or wear your homeland on your sleeve like a badge. If you're looking for inspiration, consider a few of the keywords here.

Place of Origin Name:

....

Location Type:

- Plains
- Forest
- Tundra
- Coast
- City
- Settlement
- Island
- Swamp
- Hills
- Mountains
- Castle/Fort
- Plane
- Planet
- Colony
- ....
- ....

Location Description (check all that apply):

- Shimmering
- Battle-Ravaged
- Silent
- Fetid
- Noble

- Drowned
- Fae
- Calm
- Unsullied
- Stony
- Infested
- Pastoral
- Sunny
- Hardscrabble
- Enchanted
- Bustling
- Burning
- Eternal
- Vanishing
- Dead
- Broken
- Deep
- Whispering
- Forgotten
- Ruined
- Shadowy
- Windswept
- Verdant
- ....
- ....

PHYSICAL DESCRIPTION

You can convey a great deal about your character with little more than body language. Shy and slight, cloaked against the shadows? Or burly and imposing, rattling the ground you walk on? How do you make an impression without a word?

Species/Subspecies:

....

Height: ....

Weight: ....

Build:...

Eye Color: ....

Body Texture:

- Skin
- Hair
- Fur
- Feather
- Scale
- ....
- ....

Coloring:

....

....

Other Defining Traits:

....

....

....

....

....

....

....

....

....

....

....

Defining Physical Traits:

- Battle Scar:

....

....

....

- War Wound:

....

....

....

- Striking Feature:

....

....

....

- Magical Mutation:

....

....

....

- Curious Affectation:

....

....

....

- Mystic Special Effects:

....

....

....

- Tattoos or Scarification:

....

....

....

- Bestial Attributes:

....

....

....

- Jewelry and Piercings:

....

....

....

PERSONALITY

What are the day-to-day attitudes that you bring to your party and your work? Are you fun to be around? Honest and headstrong? Select all that apply.

- Pleasant
- Angry
- Morose
- Forthright
- Flamboyant
- Quiet
- Kind

- Reserved
- Outgoing
- Proud
- Selfish
- Devious
- Clever
- Witty

- Guarded
- Trusting
- Suspicious
- Sunny
- Earnest
- Withdrawn
- Lazy

- Meticulous
- Overconfident
- Modest
- Caring
- Fun
- Pessimistic
- Candid

Do you get along well with your traveling companions?

....
....
....
....
....
....
....
....
....
....

How do you react to strangers and potential foes?

....
....
....
....
....
....
....
....
....
....

ADDITIONAL CHARACTER DESCRIPTION NOTES

....
....
....
....
....
....
....
....
....
....
....

HISTORY AND BACKSTORY

Here you'll put into words the past that you've left behind as your character steps forward into the larger world of the game. Does the past haunt you? Are you followed by the remnants of a life you long to escape? Or do you miss the simplicity of the days before you stepped out onto your road? By detailing your history, you provide a map of how you'll interact with the game world now and in the future.

FAMILY BACKGROUND

Everyone comes from somewhere, even if they technically come from no one. Use this space to list your family and their status.

Father's Name: ....

Father Is:

☐ Living   ☐ Deceased   ☐ Unknown

☐ ....

....

☐ ....

Mother's Name: ....

Mother Is:

☐ Living   ☐ Deceased   ☐ Unknown

☐ ....

....

☐ ....

Spouse/Partner Name:

....

Sibling Names and Birth Order:

....

....

....

....

....

Children/Grandchildren Names:

....

....

....

....

....

....

Other Family or Notable Figures' Names:

....

....

....

....

....

What influence did your family have on who you have become?

....

....

....

....

....

....

....

....

FAMILY DRAMA

A great way to build hooks and intrigue is to add some family drama that you've left behind or that still haunts you to this day. Check the list items that correspond with your character.

- A sibling fell to evil long ago. You still feel a sense of responsibility when their predation affects those you know.

- You were stolen away from a loving home as a babe and raised secretly for some evil purpose. You still wonder about your original family.

- You're next in line to the throne somewhere, which explains why assassins keep showing up.

- Your parents were replaced by something unnatural when you were small. Somehow you escaped, but you've been weary and perceptive ever since.

- You were raised by a family of another species, leaving you steeped in their culture and a little less comfortable in your own.

- You lost a great love once. You were even considering settling down. But they vanished, and that loss still drives you.

- Your family is a long lineage of a single proud work, but you never had the hands or stomach for the family business. Perhaps they still resent you for abandoning the tradition.

- No childhood trauma befell you or your family. You grew up peacefully and happy, content with your parents and siblings around you. Several are still among us, and you visit them for a source of strength to this day.

- ....

- ....

WEALTH STATUS

Are you living the high life, or is a rougher path for you at the moment? For some adventurers, this answer can change with ease; they find themselves rolling high after a big score, then scrabble to pay for lodging while seeking out the next job. Here, focus on your character's ideal wealth status. Where on the social strata are they the most comfortable?

- **Contented Pauper:** Scruffy, rough, and cheap even in the best of times.

- **Lean Adventurer:** Always ready to head out; it's always been about the fights instead of the scores.

- **Easy Come, Easy Goer:** You rise to the level money can buy, sleeping in barns with the same comfort as luxury suites.

- **Canny Mercantilist:** Adventure is a second business to you, and you carry wares wherever you go, offering goods and services to towns as you cross them. As such, you're usually comfortable and can expect favorable service and rates from your fellow merchant peers.

- **Savvy Grifter:** You always seem to be comfortable as long as there are enough suckers and marks in the area. The speed of your smile and wit are bested only by the speed at which you leave town.

- **Scion of Success:** Maybe your pockets are empty at the moment, but everyone knows your family has full coffers. Given your vaunted status, it would be unseemly to sleep rough.

- **High Roller:** Money is as important to you as food and water. Even in hard times, you always seem to have the little extra amenities.

- ....

....

....

HEROIC BEGINNING

There comes a time in every hero's life when they must accept that they are no longer the person they were yesterday—that they can't go back. What did your moment look like? When you stepped out the door and into a larger world, was it voluntary, or were you pushed? In the following list, you'll find a few examples of common steps that take adventurers from an old life to a new one. Choose one or make up your own.

- **Marching to Battle:** You signed up to defend your home, country, or way of life, and marched from home to war. Then you watched someone die and it changed everything.

- **Apprenticeship's End:** It was a grueling education, but even more so an abrupt end, shoved out the door with nothing but the clothes on your back and the rudimentary tools of a trade. You returned home once, but it had vanished from the face of the world.

- **Local Hero:** You weren't trained for it, but when doom befell your home, you rushed to help rather than cower and wait. Now you live for that same rush. However, you were struck by a dangerous curse.

- **Call of the Wild:** You always felt more comfortable away from the smell and noise of the crowd, and the adventurer path gave you the freedom to live outside the walls. You fell in love along the path to adventure.

- **Last Survivor:** You used to be happy, living among your kin in your hometown. But that's all gone now. Unmoored and hardened, you turned to a wandering life. Your simple journey became complicated as you mistakenly stepped into another world.

- **Lying Low:** Your last job didn't go so well. It should've been a perfect score, but the guards had changed, or you didn't see that trap. Now, shamed and wanted, you can't go home, and need to get away with your skin. You found a mystic relic early on, and your fortunes have been shaped around it.

- **An Unexpected Meeting:** You found someone or something in the shadows that offered you a bargain. A short-term job that seems to go on forever, or power at a price. You wonder if you should have said no. You lived when all signs, mystical or practical, suggest you should have died.

- **The Quest:** You set out with a single mission burning in your heart. To vanquish one foe. To retrieve one relic. Perhaps you've yet to do so, or perhaps you've completed that mission, but there are always new quests. You found the first wanted poster with your face on it a day after you walked away from home.

....
....
....
....
....
....
....
....
....
....
....
....
....
....
....

MOTIVATIONS

At a primal level, something calls every adventurer and hero to action. Understanding what drives your character to venture forth every day can help you steer decisions over the course of the game. Choose one of these lists and mark which of the options applies to your character.

Looking out for the little guy

- Used to be the little guy
- Used to be the bully
- Failed to defend someone in the past
- ....
- ....
- ....
- ....

Seeking fame and fortune

- Left a hardscrabble existence on hope
- Always felt big things were coming
- Wants the world to know your name
- ....
- ....
- ....
- ....

Called to adventure by the gods

- You've been chosen since childhood and groomed for this
- Inspiration came in the form of a vision on the battlefield
- You've sought out the forgiveness of the gods in atonement for a previous life of transgression
- ....
- ....
- ....
- ....

Avenging a wrong

- It's a personal vendetta the world doesn't know about
- You seek to stop a great evil that threatens all
- You already avenged the wrong and are seeking new purpose
- ....
- ....
- ....
- ....

A perilous path to power

- You've made a dark trade, and collection on your debt will come someday
- The power you've attained came at a dire cost to your body and mind
- You've left a trail of crimes behind you that you must always run from
- ....
- ....
- ....
- ....

Following your hero's footsteps

- Your hero was the hero of your people—many follow in their footsteps; few succeed
- Someone saved your life once, and you are compelled not to waste that gift
- Your hero may have fallen but you have learned from their example all the same
- ....
- ....
- ....
- ....

Following a trusted friend

- Childhood friends for life
- Your mentor vanished, leaving only cryptic clues
- The spirit of a fallen compatriot spurs you onward

Displaced from home

- You still hold a grudge against those who destroyed your old life
- You were separated from your home by disaster
- You earned your banishment and bear that shame

Trained for combat but the war is over

- Selling your sword arm beats life on the farm
- The war may be over but you haven't forgotten or forgiven
- You developed a taste for conflict and seek it out to this day

GEAR AND OTHER ITEMS OF INTEREST

Whether you're considering the basics, like fifty feet of silken rope plus flint and tinder, or the truly unique, like the enchanted eye of the last green dragon or a hot-rodded custom star-fighter, the trappings you carry around convey a story, and that story can be as simple or as complex as your own history. In this section, list your weapons, equipment, and miscellaneous items you possess or have decided to bring with you.

GEAR

Consider the general state of your belongings. Are you a fastidious adventurer who keeps each item organized, clean, and in good working order? Do you let things fall into messy disrepair, counting on good fortune and jerry-rigging to keep your tools useful?

Weapons

Did you begin your adventuring career with the only weapon you'll ever need? A trusted heirloom or sainted magic relic that will see you through all hardship? Or do you replace weapons with the ease of breathing, always seeking the next upgrade? Here, you'll detail your favorite weapons and your relationship to them.

Secondary Weapons

Even the most stringent devotee to the arts of the blade may carry more than one weapon, just in case. Here, list any other weapons you carry or have gathered on the journey.

Weapon (circle one)	Name	Model	Stats and Bonuses	History
primary secondary				
primary secondary				
primary secondary				
primary secondary				
primary secondary				
primary secondary				
primary secondary				

Gear Goals

It's not often that you get the chance to start the game with everything you want, and it doesn't matter if your target is something you need for quest purposes or just a wizard staff you happen to think looks particularly good with your current hat: A large part of adventuring is heading out to get what you want. So, think about just that: what you want. This space can serve as a reminder, a wish list for an interested game master (GM), or just a set of goals to put out in the world.

Item	Description	Probable Location

Gear Relationship

- Nothing but the weapons and the clothes on your back
- Packed for emergencies
- Packed for comfort
- Prepared for everything
- Compulsive collector
- ....

Storage Style

- Organized
- Untidy
- Stored in pouches and straps
- Carried by underlings
- Stored in otherspace
- Kept in the saddlebags
- Hidden on yourself
- ....

Gear Appearance

- Neglected
- Piecemeal
- Rusted
- Stolen
- Handcrafted
- Heirloom
- Store-bought
- Polished
- Customized
- Mystical
- ....

TREASURED BELONGINGS

There's always room on your character sheet for the basics, but not every piece of equipment you're carrying is basic. Here you can list the things that have real significance and importance, whether that be to the campaign at large or just to you. Whether it's as simple as a locket with a photo or as epic as the only rock left of your demolished home world, certain items are just more important.

Item:	
Description	Origin
	▦ Birthright ▦ Crafted ▦ Claimed ▦ Reward ▦ Discovered ▦ Other: ▦ Stole .... ▦ Purchased ....

Item:	
Description	Origin
	▦ Birthright ▦ Crafted ▦ Claimed ▦ Reward ▦ Discovered ▦ Other: ▦ Stole .... ▦ Purchased ....

Item:	
Description	Origin
	▦ Birthright ▦ Crafted ▦ Claimed ▦ Reward ▦ Discovered ▦ Other: ▦ Stole .... ▦ Purchased ....

Item:	
Description	**Origin**
	▨ Birthright ▨ Crafted ▨ Claimed ▨ Reward ▨ Discovered ▨ Other: ▨ Stole ▨ Purchased ....

Item:	
Description	**Origin**
	▨ Birthright ▨ Crafted ▨ Claimed ▨ Reward ▨ Discovered ▨ Other: ▨ Stole ▨ Purchased ....

Item:	
Description	**Origin**
	▨ Birthright ▨ Crafted ▨ Claimed ▨ Reward ▨ Discovered ▨ Other: ▨ Stole ▨ Purchased ....

Item:	
Description	**Origin**
	▨ Birthright ▨ Crafted ▨ Claimed ▨ Reward ▨ Discovered ▨ Other: ▨ Stole ▨ Purchased ....

PROPERTY

Have you come into possession of something large enough that it requires titles and deeds, as well as maintenance or even a constant staff for upkeep? Perhaps a secret lair, an office for your paranormal investigations, a starcruiser, or a beat-up car that'll get from point A to B if you baby it enough? When you take ownership of conveyance or property, record it here.

Property Type:

▪ Vehicle/Steed   ▪ Country
▪ Home   ▪ Planet
▪ Business   ▪ ....
▪ Town/City
▪ Kingdom   ▪ ....

Property Location: ....
....
....

Description: ....
....
....

Condition: ....
....
....

Property Type:

▪ Vehicle/Steed   ▪ Country
▪ Home   ▪ Planet
▪ Business   ▪ ....
▪ Town/City
▪ Kingdom   ▪ ....

Property Location: ....
....
....

Description: ....
....
....

Condition: ....
....
....

ADDITIONAL ITEM NOTES

....
....
....
....
....
....
....
....
....
....
....
....
....
....
....
....
....
....
....
....
....
....
....
....
....
....
....
....
....
....
....
....
....
....
....
....
....
....
....
....

ABILITIES OF NOTE

As you progress through your game world, you'll become ever more competent at your chosen field(s). Warriors become stronger and more tactically capable; casters add an ever-increasing array of arcane and divine tricks to their arsenal; negotiators become increasingly versed in matters of diplomacy and discussion; and so on. Here you'll record a list of your most efficacious and incredible abilities, along with notes describing how you personalize them to make them truly yours.

SIGNATURE ABILITIES

A perfect blade swing that can cut through the air itself. A softly spoken word that can divert the course of an empire. A granted miracle that calls down heaven itself to cast away the dead. Many characters will come to be known for such incredible feats, and those signature techniques they have will bear their names into legend.

Skill Name:	▨ Physical ▨ Divine ▨ Technological ▨ Mental ▨ Social ▨ .... ▨ Magical ▨ Artifact ▨		
Skill Effect:	Personal Upgrades:		Element Change:
Increased Range:	Increased Power:		Visual Special Effects:
Power Source (check one): ▨ Innate:	▨ Taught:		▨ Bestowed:
▨ Upgrade:	▨ Other:		▨ Other:

Skill Name:	▢ Physical ▢ Divine ▢ Technological ▢ Mental ▢ Social ▢ ▢ Magical ▢ Artifact ▢

Skill Effect:	Personal Upgrades:	Element Change:

Increased Range:	Increased Power:	Visual Special Effects:

Power Source (check one):

▢ Innate:	▢ Taught:	▢ Bestowed:
▢ Upgrade:	▢ Other:	▢ Other:

Skill Name:	▢ Physical ▢ Divine ▢ Technological ▢ Mental ▢ Social ▢ ▢ Magical ▢ Artifact ▢

Skill Effect:	Personal Upgrades:	Element Change:

Increased Range:	Increased Power:	Visual Special Effects:

Power Source (check one):

▢ Innate:	▢ Taught:	▢ Bestowed:
▢ Upgrade:	▢ Other:	▢ Other:

124

COMPLETE TOOL KIT

Adventurers may make their legacy on the flash and drama of their most powerful tools, but they survive long enough to earn that legacy through growth and maintenance of a suite of survival, combat, and social tools ranging from beginners' survival tools to expert techniques.

Skill Name:	Skill Name:	Skill Name:	Skill Name:	Skill Name:
Type: ▣ Technique ▣ Spell ▣ Power ▣ ...... ▣	Type: ▣ Technique ▣ Spell ▣ Power ▣ ...... ▣	Type: ▣ Technique ▣ Spell ▣ Power ▣ ...... ▣	Type: ▣ Technique ▣ Spell ▣ Power ▣ ...... ▣	Type: ▣ Technique ▣ Spell ▣ Power ▣ ...... ▣ ......
Description	Description	Description	Description	Description
Stats and Bonuses	Stats and Bonuses	Stats and Bonuses	Stats and Bonuses	Stats and Bonuses
Special Effects	Special Effects	Special Effects	Special Effects	Special Effects

NON-PLAYER CHARACTERS

Nobody goes through life without making some connections with the people around them, and your character should be no different. Whether it's someone you consider as close to you as a member of your own family, or a simple shop owner that you know has the best prices in town, these are the folks around you that mean the most.

CHARACTER

Character Name: ....

Character Type:

- Government Official/Politician
- Business Owner
- Family Member
- Non-Party Adventurer
- Faction or Gang Leader
- Guard/Soldier
- Refugee/Person in Need
- Old Friend
- Teacher/Expert
- Monster
- Courier
- Child/Youth
- Extraplanar/Extraplanetary Visitor
- ....
- ....

Relationship:

- Friendly
- Transactional
- Competitive
- Adversarial
- Violent
- ....
- ....

Physical Description: ....

....

....

....

....

Character Personality:

- Shifty. Paranoid. Always looking around.
- Boisterous. Welcoming. Calls you "friend."
- Serious. All business. No sense of humor.
- Friendly. Gentle. Likes being helpful.
- Cowardly. Whiny. Hates being called on.
- Gruff. Grumpy. Grudgingly does business with you.
- Greedy. Slick. In it for the profit.
- Flirty. Charming. Makes you feel special.
- Bombastic. Dramatic. All eyes on them.
- ....
- ....
- ....
- ....

What They Can Do for You:

- Has your back in any adventure
- Provides mentorship and guidance
- Boosts your ego with praise and admiration
- Always has the latest gossip
- Buys or sells contraband and rare items
- Knows when big crimes are happening
- Can introduce you to people you need
- Sells discounted goods
- Owes you an undetermined favor
- Gives you a place to crash and lie low
- Can get you the information you need
- Gets anything/anyone where it needs to go
- ....
- ....
- ....

OTHER CHARACTERS OF NOTE

There are plenty of people in the world that you hear of but don't directly interact with. The name of the local governor that might come in handy lately. The employer who sent you on your latest job. Even the bartender at your favorite hangout might be worth remembering and coming back to. Feel free to jot down anyone that feels important to remember.

ADDITIONAL NPC NOTES

127

CAMPAIGN NOTES

Herein lies your opportunity to record the great (and the infamous) deeds of your character and their journey. As they grow in power and glory, you'll be able to document each slain foe and each well-met hero on your road, and reflect back on the early days of your starting career. Additionally, it never hurts to keep a record, in case you forget an important name or person who will assuredly crop up later.

PARTY MEMBERS

It's rare that you'll venture forth to adventure alone. Who watches your back? Do you trust them implicitly or do you keep one eye open? You can list the important events and interactions here, or note down the small details to call up again when role-playing in the future.

IMPORTANT EVENTS

How have you made your mark on the world? When the lyricists compose your ode, what stories will they lean on, and what dark paths and mistakes will they carefully elide? Be sure to mention the people you met along the way too, since you never know when they'll turn up again.

BATTLES

There's certainly no reason you can't use this section as a hunting journal or scoreboard, simply listing the types and vitals of every orc or space bug you dispatch. But you might also want to focus on the epic events, the villains that brought you to the edge of doom, or the moments of good fortune or tactical brilliance that make the best boastful brags.

Battle:

Notable Foes	Treasure Acquired

Resolution:

▨ Victory
▨ Defeat
▨ ....
....
▨ ....
....

Notes and Details

Battle:

Notable Foes	Treasure Acquired

Resolution:

▨ Victory
▨ Defeat
▨ ....
....
▨ ....
....

Notes and Details

Battle:

Notable Foes	Treasure Acquired

Resolution:

▨ Victory
▨ Defeat
▨ ....
....
▨ ....
....

Notes and Details

Battle:	Notable Foes	Treasure Acquired
Resolution: ▪ Victory ▪ Defeat ▪ .... ▪		
	Notes and Details	

Battle:	Notable Foes	Treasure Acquired
Resolution: ▪ Victory ▪ Defeat ▪ .... ▪		
	Notes and Details	

Battle:	Notable Foes	Treasure Acquired
Resolution: ▪ Victory ▪ Defeat ▪ .... ▪		
	Notes and Details	

ENCOUNTERS

Not every obstacle on your journey can or will be resolved at the edge of a blade. You might perform some great feat of diplomacy, explore a new and undiscovered land, meet some of the luminaries and famous warriors of your world, or encounter any number of other incredible experiences.

ADDITIONAL CAMPAIGN NOTES

CHARACTER SIX

Character Name

Remember, you can create a character any time, but it takes investment to make them yours. Spend some time thinking about your character—not only their appearance and gear, but also their backstory and their psychology. How will they react in a given situation? This is a great place to start.

CHARACTER NAME AND DESCRIPTION

To begin, you'll detail your character's name and appearance, which is what you'll reference when describing them to other players. Go big and be distinctive! The best characters are the most memorable, and bold decisions when building your look are a great place to begin. And remember: Just because you're starting your game doesn't mean your character only just popped into existence. A few nicknames, epithets, and quirks now will go a long way in the future.

CHARACTER NAME

What's in a name? Potential, for a start. Your character's name can say a lot about them, reflecting their parentage, species, nation, and calling, all while conveying brutality, beauty, or mystery.

Full Name: ....

Known Aliases/Nicknames:

....

....

....

Titles Earned:

....

....

....

Draw your character here:

PLACE OF ORIGIN

Can folks tell where you hail from just by your gait or the cut of your hair? You might be a blank slate or wear your homeland on your sleeve like a badge. If you're looking for inspiration, consider a few of the keywords here.

Place of Origin Name:

....

Location Type:

- Plains
- Forest
- Tundra
- Coast
- City
- Settlement
- Island
- Swamp
- Hills
- Mountains
- Castle/Fort
- Plane
- Planet
- Colony
- ....
- ....

Location Description (check all that apply):

- Shimmering
- Battle-Ravaged
- Silent
- Fetid
- Noble
- Drowned
- Fae
- Calm
- Unsullied
- Stony
- Infested
- Pastoral
- Sunny
- Hardscrabble
- Enchanted
- Bustling
- Burning
- Eternal
- Vanishing
- Dead
- Broken
- Deep
- Whispering
- Forgotten
- Ruined
- Shadowy
- Windswept
- Verdant
- ....
- ....

PHYSICAL DESCRIPTION

You can convey a great deal about your character with little more than body language. Shy and slight, cloaked against the shadows? Or burly and imposing, rattling the ground you walk on? How do you make an impression without a word?

Species/Subspecies:

....

Height: ....

Weight: ....

Build: ....

Eye Color: ....

Body Texture:

- ▪ Skin
- ▪ Hair
- ▪ Fur
- ▪ Feather
- ▪ Scale
- ▪ ....
- ▪ ....

Coloring:

....

....

Other Defining Traits:

....

....

....

....

....

....

....

....

....

....

....

Defining Physical Traits:

▪ Battle Scar:

....

....

....

▪ War Wound:

....

....

....

▪ Striking Feature:

....

....

....

▪ Magical Mutation:

....

....

....

▪ Curious Affectation:

....

....

....

▪ Mystic Special Effects:

....

....

....

▪ Tattoos or Scarification:

....

....

....

▪ Bestial Attributes:

....

....

....

▪ Jewelry and Piercings:

....

....

....

PERSONALITY

What are the day-to-day attitudes that you bring to your party and your work? Are you fun to be around? Honest and headstrong? Select all that apply.

- Pleasant
- Angry
- Morose
- Forthright
- Flamboyant
- Quiet
- Kind

- Reserved
- Outgoing
- Proud
- Selfish
- Devious
- Clever
- Witty

- Guarded
- Trusting
- Suspicious
- Sunny
- Earnest
- Withdrawn
- Lazy

- Meticulous
- Overconfident
- Modest
- Caring
- Fun
- Pessimistic
- Candid

Do you get along well with your traveling companions?

How do you react to strangers and potential foes?

ADDITIONAL CHARACTER DESCRIPTION NOTES

HISTORY AND BACKSTORY

Here you'll put into words the past that you've left behind as your character steps forward into the larger world of the game. Does the past haunt you? Are you followed by the remnants of a life you long to escape? Or do you miss the simplicity of the days before you stepped out onto your road? By detailing your history, you provide a map of how you'll interact with the game world now and in the future.

FAMILY BACKGROUND

Everyone comes from somewhere, even if they technically come from no one. Use this space to list your family and their status.

Father's Name: ....

Father Is:

▪ Living   ▪ Deceased   ▪ Unknown

▪

....

▪

....

Mother's Name: ....

Mother Is:

▪ Living   ▪ Deceased   ▪ Unknown

▪

....

▪

....

Spouse/Partner Name:

....

Sibling Names and Birth Order:

....

....

....

....

....

Children/Grandchildren Names:

....

....

....

....

....

....

....

Other Family or Notable Figures' Names:

....

....

....

....

....

....

What influence did your family have on who you have become?

....

....

....

....

....

....

....

....

FAMILY DRAMA

A great way to build hooks and intrigue is to add some family drama that you've left behind or that still haunts you to this day. Check the list items that correspond with your character.

- A sibling fell to evil long ago. You still feel a sense of responsibility when their predation affects those you know.

- You were stolen away from a loving home as a babe and raised secretly for some evil purpose. You still wonder about your original family.

- You're next in line to the throne somewhere, which explains why assassins keep showing up.

- Your parents were replaced by something unnatural when you were small. Somehow you escaped, but you've been weary and perceptive ever since.

- You were raised by a family of another species, leaving you steeped in their culture and a little less comfortable in your own.

- You lost a great love once. You were even considering settling down. But they vanished, and that loss still drives you.

- Your family is a long lineage of a single proud work, but you never had the hands or stomach for the family business. Perhaps they still resent you for abandoning the tradition.

- No childhood trauma befell you or your family. You grew up peacefully and happy, content with your parents and siblings around you. Several are still among us, and you visit them for a source of strength to this day.

- ....

....

....

WEALTH STATUS

Are you living the high life, or is a rougher path for you at the moment? For some adventurers, this answer can change with ease; they find themselves rolling high after a big score, then scrabble to pay for lodging while seeking out the next job. Here, focus on your character's ideal wealth status. Where on the social strata are they the most comfortable?

- **Contented Pauper:** Scruffy, rough, and cheap even in the best of times.

- **Lean Adventurer:** Always ready to head out; it's always been about the fights instead of the scores.

- **Easy Come, Easy Goer:** You rise to the level money can buy, sleeping in barns with the same comfort as luxury suites.

- **Canny Mercantilist:** Adventure is a second business to you, and you carry wares wherever you go, offering goods and services to towns as you cross them. As such, you're usually comfortable and can expect favorable service and rates from your fellow merchant peers.

- **Savvy Grifter:** You always seem to be comfortable as long as there are enough suckers and marks in the area. The speed of your smile and wit are bested only by the speed at which you leave town.

- **Scion of Success:** Maybe your pockets are empty at the moment, but everyone knows your family has full coffers. Given your vaunted status, it would be unseemly to sleep rough.

- **High Roller:** Money is as important to you as food and water. Even in hard times, you always seem to have the little extra amenities.

- ....

....

....

HEROIC BEGINNING

There comes a time in every hero's life when they must accept that they are no longer the person they were yesterday—that they can't go back. What did your moment look like? When you stepped out the door and into a larger world, was it voluntary, or were you pushed? In the following list, you'll find a few examples of common steps that take adventurers from an old life to a new one. Choose one or make up your own.

- **Marching to Battle:** You signed up to defend your home, country, or way of life, and marched from home to war. Then you watched someone die and it changed everything.

- **Apprenticeship's End:** It was a grueling education, but even more so an abrupt end, shoved out the door with nothing but the clothes on your back and the rudimentary tools of a trade. You returned home once, but it had vanished from the face of the world.

- **Local Hero:** You weren't trained for it, but when doom befell your home, you rushed to help rather than cower and wait. Now you live for that same rush. However, you were struck by a dangerous curse.

- **Call of the Wild:** You always felt more comfortable away from the smell and noise of the crowd, and the adventurer path gave you the freedom to live outside the walls. You fell in love along the path to adventure.

- **Last Survivor:** You used to be happy, living among your kin in your hometown. But that's all gone now. Unmoored and hardened, you turned to a wandering life. Your simple journey became complicated as you mistakenly stepped into another world.

- **Lying Low:** Your last job didn't go so well. It should've been a perfect score, but the guards had changed, or you didn't see that trap. Now, shamed and wanted, you can't go home, and need to get away with your skin. You found a mystic relic early on, and your fortunes have been shaped around it.

- **An Unexpected Meeting:** You found someone or something in the shadows that offered you a bargain. A short-term job that seems to go on forever, or power at a price. You wonder if you should have said no. You lived when all signs, mystical or practical, suggest you should have died.

- **The Quest:** You set out with a single mission burning in your heart. To vanquish one foe. To retrieve one relic. Perhaps you've yet to do so, or perhaps you've completed that mission, but there are always new quests. You found the first wanted poster with your face on it a day after you walked away from home.

....
....
....
....
....
....
....
....
....
....
....
....
....
....

MOTIVATIONS

At a primal level, something calls every adventurer and hero to action. Understanding what drives your character to venture forth every day can help you steer decisions over the course of the game. Choose one of these lists and mark which of the options applies to your character.

- Looking out for the little guy
  - Used to be the little guy
  - Used to be the bully
  - Failed to defend someone in the past
  - ....
    ....
  - ....
    ....

- Seeking fame and fortune
  - Left a hardscrabble existence on hope
  - Always felt big things were coming
  - Wants the world to know your name
  - ....
    ....
  - ....
    ....

- Called to adventure by the gods
  - You've been chosen since childhood and groomed for this
  - Inspiration came in the form of a vision on the battlefield
  - You've sought out the forgiveness of the gods in atonement for a previous life of transgression
  - ....
    ....
  - ....
    ....

- Avenging a wrong
  - It's a personal vendetta the world doesn't know about
  - You seek to stop a great evil that threatens all
  - You already avenged the wrong and are seeking new purpose
  - ....
    ....
  - ....
    ....

- A perilous path to power
  - You've made a dark trade, and collection on your debt will come someday
  - The power you've attained came at a dire cost to your body and mind
  - You've left a trail of crimes behind you that you must always run from
  - ....
    ....
  - ....
    ....

- Following your hero's footsteps
  - Your hero was the hero of your people—many follow in their footsteps; few succeed
  - Someone saved your life once, and you are compelled not to waste that gift
  - Your hero may have fallen but you have learned from their example all the same
  - ....
    ....
  - ....
    ....

ADDITIONAL HISTORY
AND BACKSTORY NOTES

Following a trusted friend

- Childhood friends for life
- Your mentor vanished, leaving only cryptic clues
- The spirit of a fallen compatriot spurs you onward
- ....
- ....

Displaced from home

- You still hold a grudge against those who destroyed your old life
- You were separated from your home by disaster
- You earned your banishment and bear that shame
- ....
- ....

Trained for combat but the war is over

- Selling your sword arm beats life on the farm
- The war may be over but you haven't forgotten or forgiven
- You developed a taste for conflict and seek it out to this day
- ....
- ....

GEAR AND OTHER ITEMS OF INTEREST

Whether you're considering the basics, like fifty feet of silken rope plus flint and tinder, or the truly unique, like the enchanted eye of the last green dragon or a hot-rodded custom starfighter, the trappings you carry around convey a story, and that story can be as simple or as complex as your own history. In this section, list your weapons, equipment, and miscellaneous items you possess or have decided to bring with you.

GEAR

Consider the general state of your belongings. Are you a fastidious adventurer who keeps each item organized, clean, and in good working order? Do you let things fall into messy disrepair, counting on good fortune and jerry-rigging to keep your tools useful?

Weapons

Did you begin your adventuring career with the only weapon you'll ever need? A trusted heirloom or sainted magic relic that will see you through all hardship? Or do you replace weapons with the ease of breathing, always seeking the next upgrade? Here, you'll detail your favorite weapons and your relationship to them.

Secondary Weapons

Even the most stringent devotee to the arts of the blade may carry more than one weapon, just in case. Here, list any other weapons you carry or have gathered on the journey.

Weapon (circle one)	Name	Model	Stats and Bonuses	History
primary secondary				
primary secondary				
primary secondary				
primary secondary				
primary secondary				
primary secondary				
primary secondary				

Gear Goals

It's not often that you get the chance to start the game with everything you want, and it doesn't matter if your target is something you need for quest purposes or just a wizard staff you happen to think looks particularly good with your current hat: A large part of adventuring is heading out to get what you want. So, think about just that: what you want. This space can serve as a reminder, a wish list for an interested game master (GM), or just a set of goals to put out in the world.

Item	Description	Probable Location

Gear Relationship

- Nothing but the weapons and the clothes on your back
- Packed for emergencies
- Packed for comfort
- Prepared for everything
- Compulsive collector
- ....

Storage Style

- Organized
- Untidy
- Stored in pouches and straps
- Carried by underlings
- Stored in otherspace
- Kept in the saddlebags
- Hidden on yourself
- ....

Gear Appearance

- Neglected
- Piecemeal
- Rusted
- Stolen
- Handcrafted
- Heirloom
- Store-bought
- Polished
- Customized
- Mystical
- ....

TREASURED BELONGINGS

There's always room on your character sheet for the basics, but not every piece of equipment you're carrying is basic. Here you can list the things that have real significance and importance, whether that be to the campaign at large or just to you. Whether it's as simple as a locket with a photo or as epic as the only rock left of your demolished home world, certain items are just more important.

Item:	
Description	Origin
	▨ Birthright ▨ Crafted ▨ Claimed ▨ Reward ▨ Discovered ▨ Other: ▨ Stole .... ▨ Purchased ....

Item:	
Description	Origin
	▨ Birthright ▨ Crafted ▨ Claimed ▨ Reward ▨ Discovered ▨ Other: ▨ Stole .... ▨ Purchased ....

Item:	
Description	Origin
	▨ Birthright ▨ Crafted ▨ Claimed ▨ Reward ▨ Discovered ▨ Other: ▨ Stole .... ▨ Purchased ....

Item:

Description	Origin
	▨ Birthright ▨ Crafted ▨ Claimed ▨ Reward ▨ Discovered ▨ Other: ▨ Stole .... ▨ Purchased ....

Item:

Description	Origin
	▨ Birthright ▨ Crafted ▨ Claimed ▨ Reward ▨ Discovered ▨ Other: ▨ Stole .... ▨ Purchased ....

Item:

Description	Origin
	▨ Birthright ▨ Crafted ▨ Claimed ▨ Reward ▨ Discovered ▨ Other: ▨ Stole .... ▨ Purchased ....

Item:

Description	Origin
	▨ Birthright ▨ Crafted ▨ Claimed ▨ Reward ▨ Discovered ▨ Other: ▨ Stole .... ▨ Purchased ....

PROPERTY

Have you come into possession of something large enough that it requires titles and deeds, as well as maintenance or even a constant staff for upkeep? Perhaps a secret lair, an office for your paranormal investigations, a starcruiser, or a beat-up car that'll get from point A to B if you baby it enough? When you take ownership of conveyance or property, record it here.

Property Type:

- Vehicle/Steed
- Home
- Business
- Town/City
- Kingdom
- Country
- Planet
- ....
- ....

Property Location: ....
....
....

Description: ....
....
....

Condition: ....
....
....

Property Type:

- Vehicle/Steed
- Home
- Business
- Town/City
- Kingdom
- Country
- Planet
- ....
- ....

Property Location: ....
....
....

Description: ....
....
....

Condition: ....
....
....

ADDITIONAL ITEM NOTES

....
....
....
....
....
....
....
....
....
....
....
....
....
....
....
....
....
....
....
....
....
....
....
....
....
....
....
....
....
....
....
....
....
....
....
....
....
....
....

ABILITIES OF NOTE

As you progress through your game world, you'll become ever more competent at your chosen field(s). Warriors become stronger and more tactically capable; casters add an ever-increasing array of arcane and divine tricks to their arsenal; negotiators become increasingly versed in matters of diplomacy and discussion; and so on. Here you'll record a list of your most efficacious and incredible abilities, along with notes describing how you personalize them to make them truly yours.

SIGNATURE ABILITIES

A perfect blade swing that can cut through the air itself. A softly spoken word that can divert the course of an empire. A granted miracle that calls down heaven itself to cast away the dead. Many characters will come to be known for such incredible feats, and those signature techniques they have will bear their names into legend.

Skill Name:	■ Physical ■ Divine ■ Technological ■ Mental ■ Social ■ .... ■ Magical ■ Artifact ■		
Skill Effect:	Personal Upgrades:		Element Change:
Increased Range:	Increased Power:		Visual Special Effects:
Power Source (check one):			
■ Innate:	■ Taught:		■ Bestowed:
■ Upgrade:	■ Other:		■ Other:

Skill Name:	■ Physical ■ Divine ■ Technological ■ Mental ■ Social ■ .... ■ Magical ■ Artifact ■ ....

Skill Effect:	Personal Upgrades:	Element Change:

Increased Range:	Increased Power:	Visual Special Effects:

Power Source (check one):

■ Innate:	■ Taught:	■ Bestowed:
■ Upgrade:	■ Other:	■ Other:

Skill Name:	■ Physical ■ Divine ■ Technological ■ Mental ■ Social ■ .... ■ Magical ■ Artifact ■ ....

Skill Effect:	Personal Upgrades:	Element Change:

Increased Range:	Increased Power:	Visual Special Effects:

Power Source (check one):

■ Innate:	■ Taught:	■ Bestowed:
■ Upgrade:	■ Other:	■ Other:

COMPLETE TOOL KIT

Adventurers may make their legacy on the flash and drama of their most powerful tools, but they survive long enough to earn that legacy through growth and maintenance of a suite of survival, combat, and social tools ranging from beginners' survival tools to expert techniques.

Skill Name:	Skill Name:	Skill Name:	Skill Name:	Skill Name:
....	....	....	....	....
Type:	Type:	Type:	Type:	Type:
▨ Technique	▨ Technique	▨ Technique	▨ Technique	▨ Technique
▨ Spell	▨ Spell	▨ Spell	▨ Spell	▨ Spell
▨ Power	▨ Power	▨ Power	▨ Power	▨ Power
▨	▨	▨	▨	▨ ....
▨	▨	▨	▨	▨ ....
Description	**Description**	**Description**	**Description**	**Description**
Stats and Bonuses	**Stats and Bonuses**	**Stats and Bonuses**	**Stats and Bonuses**	**Stats and Bonuses**
Special Effects	**Special Effects**	**Special Effects**	**Special Effects**	**Special Effects**

NON-PLAYER CHARACTERS

Nobody goes through life without making some connections with the people around them, and your character should be no different. Whether it's someone you consider as close to you as a member of your own family, or a simple shop owner that you know has the best prices in town, these are the folks around you that mean the most.

CHARACTER

Character Name: ....

Character Type:

- ▣ Government Official/Politician
- ▣ Business Owner
- ▣ Family Member
- ▣ Non-Party Adventurer
- ▣ Faction or Gang Leader
- ▣ Guard/Soldier
- ▣ Refugee/Person in Need
- ▣ Old Friend
- ▣ Teacher/Expert
- ▣ Monster
- ▣ Courier
- ▣ Child/Youth
- ▣ Extraplanar/Extraplanetary Visitor
- ▣ ....
- ▣ ....

Relationship:

- ▣ Friendly
- ▣ Transactional
- ▣ Competitive
- ▣ Adversarial
- ▣ Violent
- ▣ ....
- ▣ ....

Physical Description: ....
....
....
....
....

Character Personality:

- ▣ Shifty. Paranoid. Always looking around.
- ▣ Boisterous. Welcoming. Calls you "friend."
- ▣ Serious. All business. No sense of humor.
- ▣ Friendly. Gentle. Likes being helpful.
- ▣ Cowardly. Whiny. Hates being called on.
- ▣ Gruff. Grumpy. Grudgingly does business with you.
- ▣ Greedy. Slick. In it for the profit.
- ▣ Flirty. Charming. Makes you feel special.
- ▣ Bombastic. Dramatic. All eyes on them.
- ▣ ....
- ▣ ....
- ▣ ....
- ▣ ....

What They Can Do for You:

- ▣ Has your back in any adventure
- ▣ Provides mentorship and guidance
- ▣ Boosts your ego with praise and admiration
- ▣ Always has the latest gossip
- ▣ Buys or sells contraband and rare items
- ▣ Knows when big crimes are happening
- ▣ Can introduce you to people you need
- ▣ Sells discounted goods
- ▣ Owes you an undetermined favor
- ▣ Gives you a place to crash and lie low
- ▣ Can get you the information you need
- ▣ Gets anything/anyone where it needs to go
- ▣ ....
- ▣ ....
- ▣ ....

OTHER CHARACTERS OF NOTE

There are plenty of people in the world that you hear of but don't directly interact with. The name of the local governor that might come in handy lately. The employer who sent you on your latest job. Even the bartender at your favorite hangout might be worth remembering and coming back to. Feel free to jot down anyone that feels important to remember.

ADDITIONAL NPC NOTES

CAMPAIGN NOTES

Herein lies your opportunity to record the great (and the infamous) deeds of your character and their journey. As they grow in power and glory, you'll be able to document each slain foe and each well-met hero on your road, and reflect back on the early days of your starting career. Additionally, it never hurts to keep a record, in case you forget an important name or person who will assuredly crop up later.

PARTY MEMBERS

It's rare that you'll venture forth to adventure alone. Who watches your back? Do you trust them implicitly or do you keep one eye open? You can list the important events and interactions here, or note down the small details to call up again when role-playing in the future.

IMPORTANT EVENTS

How have you made your mark on the world? When the lyricists compose your ode, what stories will they lean on, and what dark paths and mistakes will they carefully elide? Be sure to mention the people you met along the way too, since you never know when they'll turn up again.

BATTLES

There's certainly no reason you can't use this section as a hunting journal or scoreboard, simply listing the types and vitals of every orc or space bug you dispatch. But you might also want to focus on the epic events, the villains that brought you to the edge of doom, or the moments of good fortune or tactical brilliance that make the best boastful brags.

Battle:	Notable Foes	Treasure Acquired
Resolution: ▪ Victory ▪ Defeat ▪ .... ▪		
	Notes and Details	

Battle:	Notable Foes	Treasure Acquired
Resolution: ▪ Victory ▪ Defeat ▪ .... ▪		
	Notes and Details	

Battle:	Notable Foes	Treasure Acquired
Resolution: ▪ Victory ▪ Defeat ▪ .... ▪		
	Notes and Details	

Battle:	Notable Foes	Treasure Acquired
Resolution: ▪ Victory ▪ Defeat ▪ .... ▪		
	Notes and Details	

Battle:	Notable Foes	Treasure Acquired
Resolution: ▪ Victory ▪ Defeat ▪ .... ▪		
	Notes and Details	

Battle:	Notable Foes	Treasure Acquired
Resolution: ▪ Victory ▪ Defeat ▪ .... ▪		
	Notes and Details	

ENCOUNTERS

Not every obstacle on your journey can or will be resolved at the edge of a blade. You might perform some great feat of diplomacy, explore a new and undiscovered land, meet some of the luminaries and famous warriors of your world, or encounter any number of other incredible experiences.

ADDITIONAL CAMPAIGN NOTES

CHARACTER SEVEN

Character Name

Remember, you can create a character any time, but it takes investment to make them yours. Spend some time thinking about your character—not only their appearance and gear, but also their backstory and their psychology. How will they react in a given situation? This is a great place to start.

CHARACTER NAME AND DESCRIPTION

To begin, you'll detail your character's name and appearance, which is what you'll reference when describing them to other players. Go big and be distinctive! The best characters are the most memorable, and bold decisions when building your look are a great place to begin. And remember: Just because you're starting your game doesn't mean your character only just popped into existence. A few nicknames, epithets, and quirks now will go a long way in the future.

CHARACTER NAME

What's in a name? Potential, for a start. Your character's name can say a lot about them, reflecting their parentage, species, nation, and calling, all while conveying brutality, beauty, or mystery.

Full Name: ....

Known Aliases/Nicknames:

....

....

....

Titles Earned:

....

....

....

Draw your character here:

PLACE OF ORIGIN

Can folks tell where you hail from just by your gait or the cut of your hair? You might be a blank slate or wear your homeland on your sleeve like a badge. If you're looking for inspiration, consider a few of the keywords here.

Place of Origin Name:

....

Location Type:

- ▓ Plains
- ▓ Forest
- ▓ Tundra
- ▓ Coast
- ▓ City
- ▓ Settlement
- ▓ Island
- ▓ Swamp
- ▓ Hills
- ▓ Mountains
- ▓ Castle/Fort
- ▓ Plane
- ▓ Planet
- ▓ Colony
- ▓ ....
- ▓ ....

Location Description (check all that apply):

- ▓ Shimmering
- ▓ Battle-Ravaged
- ▓ Silent
- ▓ Fetid
- ▓ Noble

- ▓ Drowned
- ▓ Fae
- ▓ Calm
- ▓ Unsullied
- ▓ Stony
- ▓ Infested
- ▓ Pastoral
- ▓ Sunny
- ▓ Hardscrabble
- ▓ Enchanted
- ▓ Bustling
- ▓ Burning
- ▓ Eternal
- ▓ Vanishing
- ▓ Dead
- ▓ Broken
- ▓ Deep
- ▓ Whispering
- ▓ Forgotten
- ▓ Ruined
- ▓ Shadowy
- ▓ Windswept
- ▓ Verdant
- ▓ ....
- ▓ ....

PHYSICAL DESCRIPTION

You can convey a great deal about your character with little more than body language. Shy and slight, cloaked against the shadows? Or burly and imposing, rattling the ground you walk on? How do you make an impression without a word?

Species/Subspecies:

....

Height: ....

Weight: ....

Build: ....

Eye Color: ....

Body Texture:

- ▪ Skin   ▪ Fur   ▪ ....
- ▪ Hair   ▪ Feather   ▪ ....
- ▪ Scale

Coloring:

....

....

Other Defining Traits:

....

....

....

....

....

....

....

....

....

....

....

Defining Physical Traits:

- ▪ Battle Scar:

....

....

....

- ▪ War Wound:

....

....

....

- ▪ Striking Feature:

....

....

....

- ▪ Magical Mutation:

....

....

....

- ▪ Curious Affectation:

....

....

....

- ▪ Mystic Special Effects:

....

....

....

- ▪ Tattoos or Scarification:

....

....

....

- ▪ Bestial Attributes:

....

....

....

- ▪ Jewelry and Piercings:

....

....

....

PERSONALITY

What are the day-to-day attitudes that you bring to your party and your work? Are you fun to be around? Honest and headstrong? Select all that apply.

- Pleasant
- Angry
- Morose
- Forthright
- Flamboyant
- Quiet
- Kind

- Reserved
- Outgoing
- Proud
- Selfish
- Devious
- Clever
- Witty

- Guarded
- Trusting
- Suspicious
- Sunny
- Earnest
- Withdrawn
- Lazy

- Meticulous
- Overconfident
- Modest
- Caring
- Fun
- Pessimistic
- Candid

Do you get along well with your traveling companions?

....
....
....
....
....
....
....
....

How do you react to strangers and potential foes?

....
....
....
....
....
....
....
....

ADDITIONAL CHARACTER DESCRIPTION NOTES

....
....
....
....
....
....
....
....
....
....
....

HISTORY AND BACKSTORY

Here you'll put into words the past that you've left behind as your character steps forward into the larger world of the game. Does the past haunt you? Are you followed by the remnants of a life you long to escape? Or do you miss the simplicity of the days before you stepped out onto your road? By detailing your history, you provide a map of how you'll interact with the game world now and in the future.

FAMILY BACKGROUND

Everyone comes from somewhere, even if they technically come from no one. Use this space to list your family and their status.

Father's Name: ....

Father Is:

▣ Living   ▣ Deceased   ▣ Unknown

▣

....

....

▣

....

Mother's Name: ....

Mother Is:

▣ Living   ▣ Deceased   ▣ Unknown

▣

....

....

▣

....

Spouse/Partner Name:

....

Sibling Names and Birth Order:

....

....

....

....

....

Children/Grandchildren Names:

....

....

....

....

....

....

....

Other Family or Notable Figures' Names:

....

....

....

....

....

What influence did your family have on who you have become?

....

....

....

....

....

....

....

FAMILY DRAMA

A great way to build hooks and intrigue is to add some family drama that you've left behind or that still haunts you to this day. Check the list items that correspond with your character.

- A sibling fell to evil long ago. You still feel a sense of responsibility when their predation affects those you know.

- You were stolen away from a loving home as a babe and raised secretly for some evil purpose. You still wonder about your original family.

- You're next in line to the throne somewhere, which explains why assassins keep showing up.

- Your parents were replaced by something unnatural when you were small. Somehow you escaped, but you've been weary and perceptive ever since.

- You were raised by a family of another species, leaving you steeped in their culture and a little less comfortable in your own.

- You lost a great love once. You were even considering settling down. But they vanished, and that loss still drives you.

- Your family is a long lineage of a single proud work, but you never had the hands or stomach for the family business. Perhaps they still resent you for abandoning the tradition.

- No childhood trauma befell you or your family. You grew up peacefully and happy, content with your parents and siblings around you. Several are still among us, and you visit them for a source of strength to this day.

- ....
  ....
  ....

WEALTH STATUS

Are you living the high life, or is a rougher path for you at the moment? For some adventurers, this answer can change with ease; they find themselves rolling high after a big score, then scrabble to pay for lodging while seeking out the next job. Here, focus on your character's ideal wealth status. Where on the social strata are they the most comfortable?

- **Contented Pauper:** Scruffy, rough, and cheap even in the best of times.

- **Lean Adventurer:** Always ready to head out; it's always been about the fights instead of the scores.

- **Easy Come, Easy Goer:** You rise to the level money can buy, sleeping in barns with the same comfort as luxury suites.

- **Canny Mercantilist:** Adventure is a second business to you, and you carry wares wherever you go, offering goods and services to towns as you cross them. As such, you're usually comfortable and can expect favorable service and rates from your fellow merchant peers.

- **Savvy Grifter:** You always seem to be comfortable as long as there are enough suckers and marks in the area. The speed of your smile and wit are bested only by the speed at which you leave town.

- **Scion of Success:** Maybe your pockets are empty at the moment, but everyone knows your family has full coffers. Given your vaunted status, it would be unseemly to sleep rough.

- **High Roller:** Money is as important to you as food and water. Even in hard times, you always seem to have the little extra amenities.

- ....
  ....
  ....

HEROIC BEGINNING

There comes a time in every hero's life when they must accept that they are no longer the person they were yesterday—that they can't go back. What did your moment look like? When you stepped out the door and into a larger world, was it voluntary, or were you pushed? In the following list, you'll find a few examples of common steps that take adventurers from an old life to a new one. Choose one or make up your own.

Marching to Battle: You signed up to defend your home, country, or way of life, and marched from home to war. Then you watched someone die and it changed everything.

Apprenticeship's End: It was a grueling education, but even more so an abrupt end, shoved out the door with nothing but the clothes on your back and the rudimentary tools of a trade. You returned home once, but it had vanished from the face of the world.

Local Hero: You weren't trained for it, but when doom befell your home, you rushed to help rather than cower and wait. Now you live for that same rush. However, you were struck by a dangerous curse.

Call of the Wild: You always felt more comfortable away from the smell and noise of the crowd, and the adventurer path gave you the freedom to live outside the walls. You fell in love along the path to adventure.

Last Survivor: You used to be happy, living among your kin in your hometown. But that's all gone now. Unmoored and hardened, you turned to a wandering life. Your simple journey became complicated as you mistakenly stepped into another world.

Lying Low: Your last job didn't go so well. It should've been a perfect score, but the guards had changed, or you didn't see that trap. Now, shamed and wanted, you can't go home, and need to get away with your skin. You found a mystic relic early on, and your fortunes have been shaped around it.

An Unexpected Meeting: You found someone or something in the shadows that offered you a bargain. A short-term job that seems to go on forever, or power at a price. You wonder if you should have said no. You lived when all signs, mystical or practical, suggest you should have died.

The Quest: You set out with a single mission burning in your heart. To vanquish one foe. To retrieve one relic. Perhaps you've yet to do so, or perhaps you've completed that mission, but there are always new quests. You found the first wanted poster with your face on it a day after you walked away from home.

....
....
....
....
....
....
....
....
....
....
....
....
....
....

MOTIVATIONS

At a primal level, something calls every adventurer and hero to action. Understanding what drives your character to venture forth every day can help you steer decisions over the course of the game. Choose one of these lists and mark which of the options applies to your character.

▪ **Looking out for the little guy**
  - ▪ Used to be the little guy
  - ▪ Used to be the bully
  - ▪ Failed to defend someone in the past
  - ▪ ....
    ....
  - ▪ ....
    ....

▪ **Seeking fame and fortune**
  - ▪ Left a hardscrabble existence on hope
  - ▪ Always felt big things were coming
  - ▪ Wants the world to know your name
  - ▪ ....
    ....
  - ▪ ....
    ....

▪ **Called to adventure by the gods**
  - ▪ You've been chosen since childhood and groomed for this
  - ▪ Inspiration came in the form of a vision on the battlefield
  - ▪ You've sought out the forgiveness of the gods in atonement for a previous life of transgression
  - ▪ ....
    ....
  - ▪ ....
    ....

▪ **Avenging a wrong**
  - ▪ It's a personal vendetta the world doesn't know about
  - ▪ You seek to stop a great evil that threatens all
  - ▪ You already avenged the wrong and are seeking new purpose
  - ▪ ....
    ....
  - ▪ ....
    ....

▪ **A perilous path to power**
  - ▪ You've made a dark trade, and collection on your debt will come someday
  - ▪ The power you've attained came at a dire cost to your body and mind
  - ▪ You've left a trail of crimes behind you that you must always run from
  - ▪ ....
    ....
  - ▪ ....
    ....

▪ **Following your hero's footsteps**
  - ▪ Your hero was the hero of your people— many follow in their footsteps; few succeed
  - ▪ Someone saved your life once, and you are compelled not to waste that gift
  - ▪ Your hero may have fallen but you have learned from their example all the same
  - ▪ ....
    ....
  - ▪ ....
    ....

ADDITIONAL HISTORY
AND BACKSTORY NOTES

- Following a trusted friend
  - Childhood friends for life
  - Your mentor vanished, leaving only cryptic clues
  - The spirit of a fallen compatriot spurs you onward
  - ....
  - ....

- Displaced from home
  - You still hold a grudge against those who destroyed your old life
  - You were separated from your home by disaster
  - You earned your banishment and bear that shame
  - ....
  - ....

- Trained for combat but the war is over
  - Selling your sword arm beats life on the farm
  - The war may be over but you haven't forgotten or forgiven
  - You developed a taste for conflict and seek it out to this day
  - ....
  - ....

GEAR AND OTHER ITEMS OF INTEREST

Whether you're considering the basics, like fifty feet of silken rope plus flint and tinder, or the truly unique, like the enchanted eye of the last green dragon or a hot-rodded custom starfighter, the trappings you carry around convey a story, and that story can be as simple or as complex as your own history. In this section, list your weapons, equipment, and miscellaneous items you possess or have decided to bring with you.

GEAR

Consider the general state of your belongings. Are you a fastidious adventurer who keeps each item organized, clean, and in good working order? Do you let things fall into messy disrepair, counting on good fortune and jerry-rigging to keep your tools useful?

Weapons

Did you begin your adventuring career with the only weapon you'll ever need? A trusted heirloom or sainted magic relic that will see you through all hardship? Or do you replace weapons with the ease of breathing, always seeking the next upgrade? Here, you'll detail your favorite weapons and your relationship to them.

Secondary Weapons

Even the most stringent devotee to the arts of the blade may carry more than one weapon, just in case. Here, list any other weapons you carry or have gathered on the journey.

Weapon (circle one)	Name	Model	Stats and Bonuses	History
primary secondary				
primary secondary				
primary secondary				
primary secondary				
primary secondary				
primary secondary				
primary secondary				

Gear Goals

It's not often that you get the chance to start the game with everything you want, and it doesn't matter if your target is something you need for quest purposes or just a wizard staff you happen to think looks particularly good with your current hat: A large part of adventuring is heading out to get what you want. So, think about just that: what you want. This space can serve as a reminder, a wish list for an interested game master (GM), or just a set of goals to put out in the world.

Item	Description	Probable Location

Gear Relationship

- Nothing but the weapons and the clothes on your back
- Packed for emergencies
- Packed for comfort
- Prepared for everything
- Compulsive collector
- ....

Storage Style

- Organized
- Untidy
- Stored in pouches and straps
- Carried by underlings
- Stored in otherspace
- Kept in the saddlebags
- Hidden on yourself
- ....

Gear Appearance

- Neglected
- Piecemeal
- Rusted
- Stolen
- Handcrafted
- Heirloom
- Store-bought
- Polished
- Customized
- Mystical
- ....

TREASURED BELONGINGS

There's always room on your character sheet for the basics, but not every piece of equipment you're carrying is basic. Here you can list the things that have real significance and importance, whether that be to the campaign at large or just to you. Whether it's as simple as a locket with a photo or as epic as the only rock left of your demolished home world, certain items are just more important.

Item:	
Description	**Origin**
	■ Birthright ■ Crafted ■ Claimed ■ Reward ■ Discovered ■ Other: ■ Stole .... ■ Purchased ....

Item:	
Description	**Origin**
	■ Birthright ■ Crafted ■ Claimed ■ Reward ■ Discovered ■ Other: ■ Stole .... ■ Purchased ....

Item:	
Description	**Origin**
	■ Birthright ■ Crafted ■ Claimed ■ Reward ■ Discovered ■ Other: ■ Stole .... ■ Purchased ....

Item:

Description	Origin
	▪ Birthright ▪ Crafted ▪ Claimed ▪ Reward ▪ Discovered ▪ Other: ▪ Stole ▪ Purchased ·················· ··················

Item:

Description	Origin
	▪ Birthright ▪ Crafted ▪ Claimed ▪ Reward ▪ Discovered ▪ Other: ▪ Stole ▪ Purchased ·················· ··················

Item:

Description	Origin
	▪ Birthright ▪ Crafted ▪ Claimed ▪ Reward ▪ Discovered ▪ Other: ▪ Stole ▪ Purchased ·················· ··················

Item:

Description	Origin
	▪ Birthright ▪ Crafted ▪ Claimed ▪ Reward ▪ Discovered ▪ Other: ▪ Stole ▪ Purchased ·················· ··················

PROPERTY

Have you come into possession of something large enough that it requires titles and deeds, as well as maintenance or even a constant staff for upkeep? Perhaps a secret lair, an office for your paranormal investigations, a starcruiser, or a beat-up car that'll get from point A to B if you baby it enough? When you take ownership of conveyance or property, record it here.

Property Type:

- ▨ Vehicle/Steed   ▨ Country
- ▨ Home   ▨ Planet
- ▨ Business
- ▨ Town/City   ▨ ....
- ▨ Kingdom   ▨ ....

Property Location: ....
....
....

Description: ....
....
....

Condition: ....
....
....

Property Type:

- ▨ Vehicle/Steed   ▨ Country
- ▨ Home   ▨ Planet
- ▨ Business
- ▨ Town/City   ▨ ....
- ▨ Kingdom   ▨ ....

Property Location: ....
....
....

Description: ....
....
....

Condition: ....
....
....

ADDITIONAL ITEM NOTES

ABILITIES OF NOTE

As you progress through your game world, you'll become ever more competent at your chosen field(s). Warriors become stronger and more tactically capable; casters add an ever-increasing array of arcane and divine tricks to their arsenal; negotiators become increasingly versed in matters of diplomacy and discussion; and so on. Here you'll record a list of your most efficacious and incredible abilities, along with notes describing how you personalize them to make them truly yours.

SIGNATURE ABILITIES

A perfect blade swing that can cut through the air itself. A softly spoken word that can divert the course of an empire. A granted miracle that calls down heaven itself to cast away the dead. Many characters will come to be known for such incredible feats, and those signature techniques they have will bear their names into legend.

Skill Name:	▪ Physical ▪ Divine ▪ Technological ▪ Mental ▪ Social ▪ .... ▪ Magical ▪ Artifact ▪		
Skill Effect:	Personal Upgrades:		Element Change:
Increased Range:	Increased Power:		Visual Special Effects:
Power Source (check one): ▪ Innate: ▪ Upgrade:	▪ Taught: ▪ Other:		▪ Bestowed: ▪ Other:

Skill Name:	▓ Physical ▓ Divine ▓ Technological
	▓ Mental ▓ Social ▓ ....
	▓ Magical ▓ Artifact ▓ ....

Skill Effect:	Personal Upgrades:	Element Change:

Increased Range:	Increased Power:	Visual Special Effects:

Power Source (check one):

▓ Innate:	▓ Taught:	▓ Bestowed:
▓ Upgrade:	▓ Other:	▓ Other:

Skill Name:	▓ Physical ▓ Divine ▓ Technological
	▓ Mental ▓ Social ▓ ....
	▓ Magical ▓ Artifact ▓ ....

Skill Effect:	Personal Upgrades:	Element Change:

Increased Range:	Increased Power:	Visual Special Effects:

Power Source (check one):

▓ Innate:	▓ Taught:	▓ Bestowed:
▓ Upgrade:	▓ Other:	▓ Other:

COMPLETE TOOL KIT

Adventurers may make their legacy on the flash and drama of their most powerful tools, but they survive long enough to earn that legacy through growth and maintenance of a suite of survival, combat, and social tools ranging from beginners' survival tools to expert techniques.

Skill Name:	Skill Name:	Skill Name:	Skill Name:	Skill Name:
Type:	Type:	Type:	Type:	Type:
▢ Technique	▢ Technique	▢ Technique	▢ Technique	▢ Technique
▢ Spell	▢ Spell	▢ Spell	▢ Spell	▢ Spell
▢ Power	▢ Power	▢ Power	▢ Power	▢ Power
▢	▢	▢	▢	▢ ....
▢	▢	▢	▢	▢ ....
Description	**Description**	**Description**	**Description**	**Description**
Stats and Bonuses	**Stats and Bonuses**	**Stats and Bonuses**	**Stats and Bonuses**	**Stats and Bonuses**
Special Effects	**Special Effects**	**Special Effects**	**Special Effects**	**Special Effects**

NON-PLAYER CHARACTERS

Nobody goes through life without making some connections with the people around them, and your character should be no different. Whether it's someone you consider as close to you as a member of your own family, or a simple shop owner that you know has the best prices in town, these are the folks around you that mean the most.

CHARACTER

Character Name: ....

Character Type:

- ▦ Government Official/Politician
- ▦ Business Owner
- ▦ Family Member
- ▦ Non-Party Adventurer
- ▦ Faction or Gang Leader
- ▦ Guard/Soldier
- ▦ Refugee/Person in Need
- ▦ Old Friend
- ▦ Teacher/Expert
- ▦ Monster
- ▦ Courier
- ▦ Child/Youth
- ▦ Extraplanar/Extraplanetary Visitor
- ▦ ....
- ▦ ....

Relationship:

- ▦ Friendly
- ▦ Transactional
- ▦ Competitive
- ▦ Adversarial
- ▦ Violent
- ▦ ....
- ▦ ....

Physical Description: ....
....
....
....
....
....

Character Personality:

- ▦ Shifty. Paranoid. Always looking around.
- ▦ Boisterous. Welcoming. Calls you "friend."
- ▦ Serious. All business. No sense of humor.
- ▦ Friendly. Gentle. Likes being helpful.
- ▦ Cowardly. Whiny. Hates being called on.
- ▦ Gruff. Grumpy. Grudgingly does business with you.
- ▦ Greedy. Slick. In it for the profit.
- ▦ Flirty. Charming. Makes you feel special.
- ▦ Bombastic. Dramatic. All eyes on them.
- ▦ ....
- ▦ ....
- ▦ ....
- ▦ ....

What They Can Do for You:

- ▦ Has your back in any adventure
- ▦ Provides mentorship and guidance
- ▦ Boosts your ego with praise and admiration
- ▦ Always has the latest gossip
- ▦ Buys or sells contraband and rare items
- ▦ Knows when big crimes are happening
- ▦ Can introduce you to people you need
- ▦ Sells discounted goods
- ▦ Owes you an undetermined favor
- ▦ Gives you a place to crash and lie low
- ▦ Can get you the information you need
- ▦ Gets anything/anyone where it needs to go
- ▦ ....
- ▦ ....
- ▦ ....
- ▦ ....

OTHER CHARACTERS OF NOTE

There are plenty of people in the world that you hear of but don't directly interact with. The name of the local governor that might come in handy lately. The employer who sent you on your latest job. Even the bartender at your favorite hangout might be worth remembering and coming back to. Feel free to jot down anyone that feels important to remember.

ADDITIONAL NPC NOTES

CAMPAIGN NOTES

Herein lies your opportunity to record the great (and the infamous) deeds of your character and their journey. As they grow in power and glory, you'll be able to document each slain foe and each well-met hero on your road, and reflect back on the early days of your starting career. Additionally, it never hurts to keep a record, in case you forget an important name or person who will assuredly crop up later.

PARTY MEMBERS

It's rare that you'll venture forth to adventure alone. Who watches your back? Do you trust them implicitly or do you keep one eye open? You can list the important events and interactions here, or note down the small details to call up again when role-playing in the future.

IMPORTANT EVENTS

How have you made your mark on the world? When the lyricists compose your ode, what stories will they lean on, and what dark paths and mistakes will they carefully elide? Be sure to mention the people you met along the way too, since you never know when they'll turn up again.

BATTLES

There's certainly no reason you can't use this section as a hunting journal or scoreboard, simply listing the types and vitals of every orc or space bug you dispatch. But you might also want to focus on the epic events, the villains that brought you to the edge of doom, or the moments of good fortune or tactical brilliance that make the best boastful brags.

Battle:		Notable Foes	Treasure Acquired
Resolution: ■ Victory ■ Defeat ■ .... ■			
		Notes and Details	

Battle:		Notable Foes	Treasure Acquired
Resolution: ■ Victory ■ Defeat ■ .... ■			
		Notes and Details	

Battle:		Notable Foes	Treasure Acquired
Resolution: ■ Victory ■ Defeat ■ .... ■			
		Notes and Details	

Battle:	Notable Foes	Treasure Acquired
Resolution:		
▣ Victory		
▣ Defeat	Notes and Details	
▣		
....		
▣		
....		

Battle:	Notable Foes	Treasure Acquired
Resolution:		
▣ Victory		
▣ Defeat	Notes and Details	
▣		
....		
▣		
....		

Battle:	Notable Foes	Treasure Acquired
Resolution:		
▣ Victory		
▣ Defeat	Notes and Details	
▣		
....		
▣		
....		

ENCOUNTERS

Not every obstacle on your journey can or will be resolved at the edge of a blade. You might perform some great feat of diplomacy, explore a new and undiscovered land, meet some of the luminaries and famous warriors of your world, or encounter any number of other incredible experiences.

ADDITIONAL CAMPAIGN NOTES

CHARACTER EIGHT

Character Name

Remember, you can create a character any time, but it takes investment to make them yours. Spend some time thinking about your character—not only their appearance and gear, but also their backstory and their psychology. How will they react in a given situation? This is a great place to start.

CHARACTER NAME AND DESCRIPTION

To begin, you'll detail your character's name and appearance, which is what you'll reference when describing them to other players. Go big and be distinctive! The best characters are the most memorable, and bold decisions when building your look are a great place to begin. And remember: Just because you're starting your game doesn't mean your character only just popped into existence. A few nicknames, epithets, and quirks now will go a long way in the future.

CHARACTER NAME

What's in a name? Potential, for a start. Your character's name can say a lot about them, reflecting their parentage, species, nation, and calling, all while conveying brutality, beauty, or mystery.

Full Name: ....

Known Aliases/Nicknames:

....

....

....

Titles Earned:

....

....

....

Draw your character here:

PLACE OF ORIGIN

Can folks tell where you hail from just by your gait or the cut of your hair? You might be a blank slate or wear your homeland on your sleeve like a badge. If you're looking for inspiration, consider a few of the keywords here.

Place of Origin Name:

....

Location Type:

- Plains
- Forest
- Tundra
- Coast
- City
- Settlement
- Island
- Swamp
- Hills
- Mountains
- Castle/Fort
- Plane
- Planet
- Colony
- ....
- ....

Location Description
(check all that apply):

- Shimmering
- Battle-Ravaged
- Silent
- Fetid
- Noble

- Drowned
- Fae
- Calm
- Unsullied
- Stony
- Infested
- Pastoral
- Sunny
- Hardscrabble
- Enchanted
- Bustling
- Burning
- Eternal
- Vanishing
- Dead
- Broken
- Deep
- Whispering
- Forgotten
- Ruined
- Shadowy
- Windswept
- Verdant
- ....
- ....

PHYSICAL DESCRIPTION

You can convey a great deal about your character with little more than body language. Shy and slight, cloaked against the shadows? Or burly and imposing, rattling the ground you walk on? How do you make an impression without a word?

Species/Subspecies:

....

Height: ....

Weight: ....

Build: ....

Eye Color: ....

Body Texture:

- Skin
- Hair
- Fur
- Feather
- Scale
- ....
- ....

Coloring:

....
....

Other Defining Traits:

....
....
....
....
....
....
....
....
....
....
....
....

Defining Physical Traits:

- Battle Scar:

....
....
....

- War Wound:

....
....
....

- Striking Feature:

....
....
....

- Magical Mutation:

....
....
....

- Curious Affectation:

....
....
....

- Mystic Special Effects:

....
....

- Tattoos or Scarification:

....
....

- Bestial Attributes:

....
....

- Jewelry and Piercings:

....
....
....

PERSONALITY

What are the day-to-day attitudes that you bring to your party and your work? Are you fun to be around? Honest and headstrong? Select all that apply.

- ▦ Pleasant
- ▦ Angry
- ▦ Morose
- ▦ Forthright
- ▦ Flamboyant
- ▦ Quiet
- ▦ Kind

- ▦ Reserved
- ▦ Outgoing
- ▦ Proud
- ▦ Selfish
- ▦ Devious
- ▦ Clever
- ▦ Witty

- ▦ Guarded
- ▦ Trusting
- ▦ Suspicious
- ▦ Sunny
- ▦ Earnest
- ▦ Withdrawn
- ▦ Lazy

- ▦ Meticulous
- ▦ Overconfident
- ▦ Modest
- ▦ Caring
- ▦ Fun
- ▦ Pessimistic
- ▦ Candid

Do you get along well with your traveling companions?

....
....
....
....
....
....
....
....
....

How do you react to strangers and potential foes?

....
....
....
....
....
....
....
....
....

ADDITIONAL CHARACTER DESCRIPTION NOTES

....
....
....
....
....
....
....
....
....
....
....

HISTORY AND BACKSTORY

Here you'll put into words the past that you've left behind as your character steps forward into the larger world of the game. Does the past haunt you? Are you followed by the remnants of a life you long to escape? Or do you miss the simplicity of the days before you stepped out onto your road? By detailing your history, you provide a map of how you'll interact with the game world now and in the future.

FAMILY BACKGROUND

Everyone comes from somewhere, even if they technically come from no one. Use this space to list your family and their status.

Father's Name: ....

Father Is:

■ Living   ■ Deceased   ■ Unknown

■ ....

■ ....

Mother's Name: ....

Mother Is:

■ Living   ■ Deceased   ■ Unknown

■ ....

■ ....

Spouse/Partner Name:

....

Sibling Names and Birth Order:

....

....

....

....

Children/Grandchildren Names:

....

....

....

....

....

....

Other Family or Notable Figures' Names:

....

....

....

....

What influence did your family have on who you have become?

....

....

....

....

....

....

....

FAMILY DRAMA

A great way to build hooks and intrigue is to add some family drama that you've left behind or that still haunts you to this day. Check the list items that correspond with your character.

- A sibling fell to evil long ago. You still feel a sense of responsibility when their predation affects those you know.

- You were stolen away from a loving home as a babe and raised secretly for some evil purpose. You still wonder about your original family.

- You're next in line to the throne somewhere, which explains why assassins keep showing up.

- Your parents were replaced by something unnatural when you were small. Somehow you escaped, but you've been weary and perceptive ever since.

- You were raised by a family of another species, leaving you steeped in their culture and a little less comfortable in your own.

- You lost a great love once. You were even considering settling down. But they vanished, and that loss still drives you.

- Your family is a long lineage of a single proud work, but you never had the hands or stomach for the family business. Perhaps they still resent you for abandoning the tradition.

- No childhood trauma befell you or your family. You grew up peacefully and happily, content with your parents and siblings around you. Several are still among us, and you visit them for a source of strength to this day.

- ....

- ....

- ....

WEALTH STATUS

Are you living the high life, or is a rougher path for you at the moment? For some adventurers, this answer can change with ease; they find themselves rolling high after a big score, then scrabble to pay for lodging while seeking out the next job. Here, focus on your character's ideal wealth status. Where on the social strata are they the most comfortable?

- **Contented Pauper:** Scruffy, rough, and cheap even in the best of times.

- **Lean Adventurer:** Always ready to head out; it's always been about the fights instead of the scores.

- **Easy Come, Easy Goer:** You rise to the level money can buy, sleeping in barns with the same comfort as luxury suites.

- **Canny Mercantilist:** Adventure is a second business to you, and you carry wares wherever you go, offering goods and services to towns as you cross them. As such, you're usually comfortable and can expect favorable service and rates from your fellow merchant peers.

- **Savvy Grifter:** You always seem to be comfortable as long as there are enough suckers and marks in the area. The speed of your smile and wit are bested only by the speed at which you leave town.

- **Scion of Success:** Maybe your pockets are empty at the moment, but everyone knows your family has full coffers. Given your vaunted status, it would be unseemly to sleep rough.

- **High Roller:** Money is as important to you as food and water. Even in hard times, you always seem to have the little extra amenities.

- ....

- ....

- ....

HEROIC BEGINNING

There comes a time in every hero's life when they must accept that they are no longer the person they were yesterday—that they can't go back. What did your moment look like? When you stepped out the door and into a larger world, was it voluntary, or were you pushed? In the following list, you'll find a few examples of common steps that take adventurers from an old life to a new one. Choose one or make up your own.

Marching to Battle: You signed up to defend your home, country, or way of life, and marched from home to war. Then you watched someone die and it changed everything.

Apprenticeship's End: It was a grueling education, but even more so an abrupt end, shoved out the door with nothing but the clothes on your back and the rudimentary tools of a trade. You returned home once, but it had vanished from the face of the world.

Local Hero: You weren't trained for it, but when doom befell your home, you rushed to help rather than cower and wait. Now you live for that same rush. However, you were struck by a dangerous curse.

Call of the Wild: You always felt more comfortable away from the smell and noise of the crowd, and the adventurer path gave you the freedom to live outside the walls. You fell in love along the path to adventure.

Last Survivor: You used to be happy, living among your kin in your hometown. But that's all gone now. Unmoored and hardened, you turned to a wandering life. Your simple journey became complicated as you mistakenly stepped into another world.

Lying Low: Your last job didn't go so well. It should've been a perfect score, but the guards had changed, or you didn't see that trap. Now, shamed and wanted, you can't go home, and need to get away with your skin. You found a mystic relic early on, and your fortunes have been shaped around it.

An Unexpected Meeting: You found someone or something in the shadows that offered you a bargain. A short-term job that seems to go on forever, or power at a price. You wonder if you should have said no. You lived when all signs, mystical or practical, suggest you should have died.

The Quest: You set out with a single mission burning in your heart. To vanquish one foe. To retrieve one relic. Perhaps you've yet to do so, or perhaps you've completed that mission, but there are always new quests. You found the first wanted poster with your face on it a day after you walked away from home.

MOTIVATIONS

At a primal level, something calls every adventurer and hero to action. Understanding what drives your character to venture forth every day can help you steer decisions over the course of the game. Choose one of these lists and mark which of the options applies to your character.

- Looking out for the little guy
  - Used to be the little guy
  - Used to be the bully
  - Failed to defend someone in the past
  - ....
  - ....
  - ....
  - ....

- Seeking fame and fortune
  - Left a hardscrabble existence on hope
  - Always felt big things were coming
  - Wants the world to know your name
  - ....
  - ....
  - ....
  - ....

- Called to adventure by the gods
  - You've been chosen since childhood and groomed for this
  - Inspiration came in the form of a vision on the battlefield
  - You've sought out the forgiveness of the gods in atonement for a previous life of transgression
  - ....
  - ....
  - ....
  - ....

- Avenging a wrong
  - It's a personal vendetta the world doesn't know about
  - You seek to stop a great evil that threatens all
  - You already avenged the wrong and are seeking new purpose
  - ....
  - ....
  - ....
  - ....

- A perilous path to power
  - You've made a dark trade, and collection on your debt will come someday
  - The power you've attained came at a dire cost to your body and mind
  - You've left a trail of crimes behind you that you must always run from
  - ....
  - ....
  - ....
  - ....

- Following your hero's footsteps
  - Your hero was the hero of your people— many follow in their footsteps; few succeed
  - Someone saved your life once, and you are compelled not to waste that gift
  - Your hero may have fallen but you have learned from their example all the same
  - ....
  - ....
  - ....
  - ....

ADDITIONAL HISTORY
AND BACKSTORY NOTES

Following a trusted friend

- Childhood friends for life
- Your mentor vanished, leaving only cryptic clues
- The spirit of a fallen compatriot spurs you onward

Displaced from home

- You still hold a grudge against those who destroyed your old life
- You were separated from your home by disaster
- You earned your banishment and bear that shame

Trained for combat but the war is over

- Selling your sword arm beats life on the farm
- The war may be over but you haven't forgotten or forgiven
- You developed a taste for conflict and seek it out to this day

GEAR AND OTHER ITEMS OF INTEREST

Whether you're considering the basics, like fifty feet of silken rope plus flint and tinder, or the truly unique, like the enchanted eye of the last green dragon or a hot-rodded custom star-fighter, the trappings you carry around convey a story, and that story can be as simple or as complex as your own history. In this section, list your weapons, equipment, and miscellaneous items you possess or have decided to bring with you.

GEAR

Consider the general state of your belongings. Are you a fastidious adventurer who keeps each item organized, clean, and in good working order? Do you let things fall into messy disrepair, counting on good fortune and jerry-rigging to keep your tools useful?

Weapons

Did you begin your adventuring career with the only weapon you'll ever need? A trusted heirloom or sainted magic relic that will see you through all hardship? Or do you replace weapons with the ease of breathing, always seeking the next upgrade? Here, you'll detail your favorite weapons and your relationship to them.

Secondary Weapons

Even the most stringent devotee to the arts of the blade may carry more than one weapon, just in case. Here, list any other weapons you carry or have gathered on the journey.

Weapon (circle one)	Name	Model	Stats and Bonuses	History
primary secondary				
primary secondary				
primary secondary				
primary secondary				
primary secondary				
primary secondary				
primary secondary				

Gear Goals

It's not often that you get the chance to start the game with everything you want, and it doesn't matter if your target is something you need for quest purposes or just a wizard staff you happen to think looks particularly good with your current hat: A large part of adventuring is heading out to get what you want. So, think about just that: what you want. This space can serve as a reminder, a wish list for an interested game master (GM), or just a set of goals to put out in the world.

Item	Description	Probable Location

Gear Relationship

- Nothing but the weapons and the clothes on your back
- Packed for emergencies
- Packed for comfort
- Prepared for everything
- Compulsive collector
- ....

Storage Style

- Organized
- Untidy
- Stored in pouches and straps
- Carried by underlings
- Stored in otherspace
- Kept in the saddlebags
- Hidden on yourself
- ....

Gear Appearance

- Neglected
- Piecemeal
- Rusted
- Stolen
- Handcrafted
- Heirloom
- Store-bought
- Polished
- Customized
- Mystical
- ....

TREASURED BELONGINGS

There's always room on your character sheet for the basics, but not every piece of equipment you're carrying is basic. Here you can list the things that have real significance and importance, whether that be to the campaign at large or just to you. Whether it's as simple as a locket with a photo or as epic as the only rock left of your demolished home world, certain items are just more important.

Item:

Description	Origin	
	▓ Birthright	▓ Crafted
	▓ Claimed	▓ Reward
	▓ Discovered	▓ Other:
	▓ Stole	....
	▓ Purchased	....

Item:

Description	Origin	
	▓ Birthright	▓ Crafted
	▓ Claimed	▓ Reward
	▓ Discovered	▓ Other:
	▓ Stole	....
	▓ Purchased	....

Item:

Description	Origin	
	▓ Birthright	▓ Crafted
	▓ Claimed	▓ Reward
	▓ Discovered	▓ Other:
	▓ Stole	....
	▓ Purchased	....

Item:

Description	Origin	
	▪ Birthright	▪ Crafted
	▪ Claimed	▪ Reward
	▪ Discovered	▪ Other:
	▪ Stole	....
	▪ Purchased	....

Item:

Description	Origin	
	▪ Birthright	▪ Crafted
	▪ Claimed	▪ Reward
	▪ Discovered	▪ Other:
	▪ Stole	....
	▪ Purchased	....

Item:

Description	Origin	
	▪ Birthright	▪ Crafted
	▪ Claimed	▪ Reward
	▪ Discovered	▪ Other:
	▪ Stole	....
	▪ Purchased	....

Item:

Description	Origin	
	▪ Birthright	▪ Crafted
	▪ Claimed	▪ Reward
	▪ Discovered	▪ Other:
	▪ Stole	....
	▪ Purchased	....

PROPERTY

Have you come into possession of something large enough that it requires titles and deeds, as well as maintenance or even a constant staff for upkeep? Perhaps a secret lair, an office for your paranormal investigations, a starcruiser, or a beat-up car that'll get from point A to B if you baby it enough? When you take ownership of conveyance or property, record it here.

Property Type:

- ▨ Vehicle/Steed
- ▨ Home
- ▨ Business
- ▨ Town/City
- ▨ Kingdom
- ▨ Country
- ▨ Planet
- ▨ ....
- ▨ ....

Property Location: ....
....

Description: ....
....

Condition: ....
....
....

Property Type:

- ▨ Vehicle/Steed
- ▨ Home
- ▨ Business
- ▨ Town/City
- ▨ Kingdom
- ▨ Country
- ▨ Planet
- ▨ ....
- ▨ ....

Property Location: ....
....

Description: ....
....

Condition: ....
....
....

ADDITIONAL ITEM NOTES

ABILITIES OF NOTE

As you progress through your game world, you'll become ever more competent at your chosen field(s). Warriors become stronger and more tactically capable; casters add an ever-increasing array of arcane and divine tricks to their arsenal; negotiators become increasingly versed in matters of diplomacy and discussion; and so on. Here you'll record a list of your most efficacious and incredible abilities, along with notes describing how you personalize them to make them truly yours.

SIGNATURE ABILITIES

A perfect blade swing that can cut through the air itself. A softly spoken word that can divert the course of an empire. A granted miracle that calls down heaven itself to cast away the dead. Many characters will come to be known for such incredible feats, and those signature techniques they have will bear their names into legend.

Skill Name:	■ Physical ■ Divine ■ Technological ■ Mental ■ Social ■ .... ■ Magical ■ Artifact ■		
Skill Effect:	Personal Upgrades:	Element Change:	
Increased Range:	Increased Power:	Visual Special Effects:	
Power Source (check one): ■ Innate: ■ Taught: ■ Bestowed: ■ Upgrade: ■ Other: ■ Other:			

195

Skill Name:	☐ Physical ☐ Divine ☐ Technological
	☐ Mental ☐ Social ☐ ....
	☐ Magical ☐ Artifact ☐ ....

Skill Effect:	Personal Upgrades:	Element Change:

Increased Range:	Increased Power:	Visual Special Effects:

Power Source (check one):

☐ Innate:	☐ Taught:	☐ Bestowed:
☐ Upgrade:	☐ Other:	☐ Other:

Skill Name:	☐ Physical ☐ Divine ☐ Technological
	☐ Mental ☐ Social ☐ ....
	☐ Magical ☐ Artifact ☐ ....

Skill Effect:	Personal Upgrades:	Element Change:

Increased Range:	Increased Power:	Visual Special Effects:

Power Source (check one):

☐ Innate:	☐ Taught:	☐ Bestowed:
☐ Upgrade:	☐ Other:	☐ Other:

COMPLETE TOOL KIT

Adventurers may make their legacy on the flash and drama of their most powerful tools, but they survive long enough to earn that legacy through growth and maintenance of a suite of survival, combat, and social tools ranging from beginners' survival tools to expert techniques.

Skill Name:	Skill Name:	Skill Name:	Skill Name:	Skill Name:
....	....	....	....	....
Type:	Type:	Type:	Type:	Type:
▓ Technique	▓ Technique	▓ Technique	▓ Technique	▓ Technique
▓ Spell	▓ Spell	▓ Spell	▓ Spell	▓ Spell
▓ Power	▓ Power	▓ Power	▓ Power	▓ Power
▓	▓	▓	▓	▓ ....
▓	▓	▓	▓	▓ ....
Description	**Description**	**Description**	**Description**	**Description**
Stats and Bonuses	**Stats and Bonuses**	**Stats and Bonuses**	**Stats and Bonuses**	**Stats and Bonuses**
Special Effects	**Special Effects**	**Special Effects**	**Special Effects**	**Special Effects**

NON-PLAYER CHARACTERS

Nobody goes through life without making some connections with the people around them, and your character should be no different. Whether it's someone you consider as close to you as a member of your own family, or a simple shop owner that you know has the best prices in town, these are the folks around you that mean the most.

CHARACTER

Character Name: ....

Character Type:

- ▣ Government Official/Politician
- ▣ Business Owner
- ▣ Family Member
- ▣ Non-Party Adventurer
- ▣ Faction or Gang Leader
- ▣ Guard/Soldier
- ▣ Refugee/Person in Need
- ▣ Old Friend
- ▣ Teacher/Expert
- ▣ Monster
- ▣ Courier
- ▣ Child/Youth
- ▣ Extraplanar/Extraplanetary Visitor
- ▣ ....
- ▣ ....

Relationship:

- ▣ Friendly
- ▣ Transactional
- ▣ Competitive
- ▣ Adversarial
- ▣ Violent
- ▣ ....
- ▣ ....

Physical Description: ....
....
....
....
....

Character Personality:

- ▣ Shifty. Paranoid. Always looking around.
- ▣ Boisterous. Welcoming. Calls you "friend."
- ▣ Serious. All business. No sense of humor.
- ▣ Friendly. Gentle. Likes being helpful.
- ▣ Cowardly. Whiny. Hates being called on.
- ▣ Gruff. Grumpy. Grudgingly does business with you.
- ▣ Greedy. Slick. In it for the profit.
- ▣ Flirty. Charming. Makes you feel special.
- ▣ Bombastic. Dramatic. All eyes on them.
- ▣ ....
- ▣ ....
- ▣ ....
- ▣ ....

What They Can Do for You:

- ▣ Has your back in any adventure
- ▣ Provides mentorship and guidance
- ▣ Boosts your ego with praise and admiration
- ▣ Always has the latest gossip
- ▣ Buys or sells contraband and rare items
- ▣ Knows when big crimes are happening
- ▣ Can introduce you to people you need
- ▣ Sells discounted goods
- ▣ Owes you an undetermined favor
- ▣ Gives you a place to crash and lie low
- ▣ Can get you the information you need
- ▣ Gets anything/anyone where it needs to go
- ▣ ....
- ▣ ....
- ▣ ....
- ▣ ....

OTHER CHARACTERS OF NOTE

There are plenty of people in the world that you hear of but don't directly interact with. The name of the local governor that might come in handy lately. The employer who sent you on your latest job. Even the bartender at your favorite hangout might be worth remembering and coming back to. Feel free to jot down anyone that feels important to remember.

ADDITIONAL NPC NOTES

CAMPAIGN NOTES

Herein lies your opportunity to record the great (and the infamous) deeds of your character and their journey. As they grow in power and glory, you'll be able to document each slain foe and each well-met hero on your road, and reflect back on the early days of your starting career. Additionally, it never hurts to keep a record, in case you forget an important name or person who will assuredly crop up later.

PARTY MEMBERS

It's rare that you'll venture forth to adventure alone. Who watches your back? Do you trust them implicitly or do you keep one eye open? You can list the important events and interactions here, or note down the small details to call up again when role-playing in the future.

IMPORTANT EVENTS

How have you made your mark on the world? When the lyricists compose your ode, what stories will they lean on, and what dark paths and mistakes will they carefully elide? Be sure to mention the people you met along the way too, since you never know when they'll turn up again.

BATTLES

There's certainly no reason you can't use this section as a hunting journal or scoreboard, simply listing the types and vitals of every orc or space bug you dispatch. But you might also want to focus on the epic events, the villains that brought you to the edge of doom, or the moments of good fortune or tactical brilliance that make the best boastful brags.

Battle:

Notable Foes	Treasure Acquired

Resolution:
- Victory
- Defeat
- ....
....
- ....
....

Notes and Details

Battle:

Notable Foes	Treasure Acquired

Resolution:
- Victory
- Defeat
- ....
....
- ....
....

Notes and Details

Battle:

Notable Foes	Treasure Acquired

Resolution:
- Victory
- Defeat
- ....
....
- ....
....

Notes and Details

Battle:	Notable Foes	Treasure Acquired
Resolution: ▦ Victory ▦ Defeat ▦ .... ▦		
	Notes and Details	

Battle:	Notable Foes	Treasure Acquired
Resolution: ▦ Victory ▦ Defeat ▦ .... ▦		
	Notes and Details	

Battle:	Notable Foes	Treasure Acquired
Resolution: ▦ Victory ▦ Defeat ▦ .... ▦		
	Notes and Details	

ENCOUNTERS

Not every obstacle on your journey can or will be resolved at the edge of a blade. You might perform some great feat of diplomacy, explore a new and undiscovered land, meet some of the luminaries and famous warriors of your world, or encounter any number of other incredible experiences.

ADDITIONAL CAMPAIGN NOTES

CHARACTER NINE

Character Name

Remember, you can create a character any time, but it takes investment to make them yours. Spend some time thinking about your character—not only their appearance and gear, but also their backstory and their psychology. How will they react in a given situation? This is a great place to start.

CHARACTER NAME AND DESCRIPTION

To begin, you'll detail your character's name and appearance, which is what you'll reference when describing them to other players. Go big and be distinctive! The best characters are the most memorable, and bold decisions when building your look are a great place to begin. And remember: Just because you're starting your game doesn't mean your character only just popped into existence. A few nicknames, epithets, and quirks now will go a long way in the future.

CHARACTER NAME

What's in a name? Potential, for a start. Your character's name can say a lot about them, reflecting their parentage, species, nation, and calling, all while conveying brutality, beauty, or mystery.

Full Name: ....

Known Aliases/Nicknames:

....

....

....

Titles Earned:

....

....

....

Draw your character here:

PLACE OF ORIGIN

Can folks tell where you hail from just by your gait or the cut of your hair? You might be a blank slate or wear your homeland on your sleeve like a badge. If you're looking for inspiration, consider a few of the keywords here.

Place of Origin Name:

....

Location Type:

- Plains
- Forest
- Tundra
- Coast
- City
- Settlement
- Island
- Swamp
- Hills
- Mountains
- Castle/Fort
- Plane
- Planet
- Colony
- ....
- ....

Location Description (check all that apply):

- Shimmering
- Battle-Ravaged
- Silent
- Fetid
- Noble
- Drowned
- Fae
- Calm
- Unsullied
- Stony
- Infested
- Pastoral
- Sunny
- Hardscrabble
- Enchanted
- Bustling
- Burning
- Eternal
- Vanishing
- Dead
- Broken
- Deep
- Whispering
- Forgotten
- Ruined
- Shadowy
- Windswept
- Verdant
- ....
- ....

PHYSICAL DESCRIPTION

You can convey a great deal about your character with little more than body language. Shy and slight, cloaked against the shadows? Or burly and imposing, rattling the ground you walk on? How do you make an impression without a word?

Species/Subspecies:

....

Height: ....

Weight: ....

Build: ....

Eye Color: ....

Body Texture:

- Skin
- Hair
- Fur
- Feather
- Scale
- ....
- ....

Coloring:

....

....

Other Defining Traits:

....

....

....

....

....

....

....

....

....

....

....

....

Defining Physical Traits:

- Battle Scar:

....

....

- War Wound:

....

....

- Striking Feature:

....

....

- Magical Mutation:

....

....

- Curious Affectation:

....

....

- Mystic Special Effects:

....

....

- Tattoos or Scarification:

....

....

- Bestial Attributes:

....

....

- Jewelry and Piercings:

....

....

....

PERSONALITY

What are the day-to-day attitudes that you bring to your party and your work? Are you fun to be around? Honest and headstrong? Select all that apply.

- ▣ Pleasant
- ▣ Angry
- ▣ Morose
- ▣ Forthright
- ▣ Flamboyant
- ▣ Quiet
- ▣ Kind

- ▣ Reserved
- ▣ Outgoing
- ▣ Proud
- ▣ Selfish
- ▣ Devious
- ▣ Clever
- ▣ Witty

- ▣ Guarded
- ▣ Trusting
- ▣ Suspicious
- ▣ Sunny
- ▣ Earnest
- ▣ Withdrawn
- ▣ Lazy

- ▣ Meticulous
- ▣ Overconfident
- ▣ Modest
- ▣ Caring
- ▣ Fun
- ▣ Pessimistic
- ▣ Candid

Do you get along well with your traveling companions?

....
....
....
....
....
....
....
....
....

How do you react to strangers and potential foes?

....
....
....
....
....
....
....
....
....

ADDITIONAL CHARACTER DESCRIPTION NOTES

....
....
....
....
....
....
....
....
....
....
....
....

HISTORY AND BACKSTORY

Here you'll put into words the past that you've left behind as your character steps forward into the larger world of the game. Does the past haunt you? Are you followed by the remnants of a life you long to escape? Or do you miss the simplicity of the days before you stepped out onto your road? By detailing your history, you provide a map of how you'll interact with the game world now and in the future.

FAMILY BACKGROUND

Everyone comes from somewhere, even if they technically come from no one. Use this space to list your family and their status.

Father's Name: ....

Father Is:

▪ Living ▪ Deceased ▪ Unknown

▪ ....

....

▪ ....

....

Mother's Name: ....

Mother Is:

▪ Living ▪ Deceased ▪ Unknown

▪ ....

....

▪ ....

....

Spouse/Partner Name:

....

Sibling Names and Birth Order:

....

....

....

....

....

Children/Grandchildren Names:

....

....

....

....

....

....

Other Family or Notable Figures' Names:

....

....

....

....

....

What influence did your family have on who you have become?

....

....

....

....

....

....

....

....

FAMILY DRAMA

A great way to build hooks and intrigue is to add some family drama that you've left behind or that still haunts you to this day. Check the list items that correspond with your character.

- A sibling fell to evil long ago. You still feel a sense of responsibility when their predation affects those you know.

- You were stolen away from a loving home as a babe and raised secretly for some evil purpose. You still wonder about your original family.

- You're next in line to the throne somewhere, which explains why assassins keep showing up.

- Your parents were replaced by something unnatural when you were small. Somehow you escaped, but you've been weary and perceptive ever since.

- You were raised by a family of another species, leaving you steeped in their culture and a little less comfortable in your own.

- You lost a great love once. You were even considering settling down. But they vanished, and that loss still drives you.

- Your family is a long lineage of a single proud work, but you never had the hands or stomach for the family business. Perhaps they still resent you for abandoning the tradition.

- No childhood trauma befell you or your family. You grew up peacefully and happy, content with your parents and siblings around you. Several are still among us, and you visit them for a source of strength to this day.

- ....

- ....

- ....

WEALTH STATUS

Are you living the high life, or is a rougher path for you at the moment? For some adventurers, this answer can change with ease; they find themselves rolling high after a big score, then scrabble to pay for lodging while seeking out the next job. Here, focus on your character's ideal wealth status. Where on the social strata are they the most comfortable?

- **Contented Pauper:** Scruffy, rough, and cheap even in the best of times.

- **Lean Adventurer:** Always ready to head out; it's always been about the fights instead of the scores.

- **Easy Come, Easy Goer:** You rise to the level money can buy, sleeping in barns with the same comfort as luxury suites.

- **Canny Mercantilist:** Adventure is a second business to you, and you carry wares wherever you go, offering goods and services to towns as you cross them. As such, you're usually comfortable and can expect favorable service and rates from your fellow merchant peers.

- **Savvy Grifter:** You always seem to be comfortable as long as there are enough suckers and marks in the area. The speed of your smile and wit are bested only by the speed at which you leave town.

- **Scion of Success:** Maybe your pockets are empty at the moment, but everyone knows your family has full coffers. Given your vaunted status, it would be unseemly to sleep rough.

- **High Roller:** Money is as important to you as food and water. Even in hard times, you always seem to have the little extra amenities.

- ....

- ....

- ....

HEROIC BEGINNING

There comes a time in every hero's life when they must accept that they are no longer the person they were yesterday—that they can't go back. What did your moment look like? When you stepped out the door and into a larger world, was it voluntary, or were you pushed? In the following list, you'll find a few examples of common steps that take adventurers from an old life to a new one. Choose one or make up your own.

- **Marching to Battle:** You signed up to defend your home, country, or way of life, and marched from home to war. Then you watched someone die and it changed everything.

- **Apprenticeship's End:** It was a grueling education, but even more so an abrupt end, shoved out the door with nothing but the clothes on your back and the rudimentary tools of a trade. You returned home once, but it had vanished from the face of the world.

- **Local Hero:** You weren't trained for it, but when doom befell your home, you rushed to help rather than cower and wait. Now you live for that same rush. However, you were struck by a dangerous curse.

- **Call of the Wild:** You always felt more comfortable away from the smell and noise of the crowd, and the adventurer path gave you the freedom to live outside the walls. You fell in love along the path to adventure.

- **Last Survivor:** You used to be happy, living among your kin in your hometown. But that's all gone now. Unmoored and hardened, you turned to a wandering life. Your simple journey became complicated as you mistakenly stepped into another world.

- **Lying Low:** Your last job didn't go so well. It should've been a perfect score, but the guards had changed, or you didn't see that trap. Now, shamed and wanted, you can't go home, and need to get away with your skin. You found a mystic relic early on, and your fortunes have been shaped around it.

- **An Unexpected Meeting:** You found someone or something in the shadows that offered you a bargain. A short-term job that seems to go on forever, or power at a price. You wonder if you should have said no. You lived when all signs, mystical or practical, suggest you should have died.

- **The Quest:** You set out with a single mission burning in your heart. To vanquish one foe. To retrieve one relic. Perhaps you've yet to do so, or perhaps you've completed that mission, but there are always new quests. You found the first wanted poster with your face on it a day after you walked away from home.

....
....
....
....
....
....
....
....
....
....
....
....
....

MOTIVATIONS

At a primal level, something calls every adventurer and hero to action. Understanding what drives your character to venture forth every day can help you steer decisions over the course of the game. Choose one of these lists and mark which of the options applies to your character.

▪ Looking out for the little guy

- ▪ Used to be the little guy
- ▪ Used to be the bully
- ▪ Failed to defend someone in the past
- ▪ ....
  ....
- ▪ ....
  ....

▪ Seeking fame and fortune

- ▪ Left a hardscrabble existence on hope
- ▪ Always felt big things were coming
- ▪ Wants the world to know your name
- ▪ ....
  ....
- ▪ ....
  ....

▪ Called to adventure by the gods

- ▪ You've been chosen since childhood and groomed for this
- ▪ Inspiration came in the form of a vision on the battlefield
- ▪ You've sought out the forgiveness of the gods in atonement for a previous life of transgression
- ▪ ....
  ....
- ▪ ....
  ....

▪ Avenging a wrong

- ▪ It's a personal vendetta the world doesn't know about
- ▪ You seek to stop a great evil that threatens all
- ▪ You already avenged the wrong and are seeking new purpose
- ▪ ....
  ....
- ▪ ....
  ....

▪ A perilous path to power

- ▪ You've made a dark trade, and collection on your debt will come someday
- ▪ The power you've attained came at a dire cost to your body and mind
- ▪ You've left a trail of crimes behind you that you must always run from
- ▪ ....
  ....
- ▪ ....
  ....

▪ Following your hero's footsteps

- ▪ Your hero was the hero of your people— many follow in their footsteps; few succeed
- ▪ Someone saved your life once, and you are compelled not to waste that gift
- ▪ Your hero may have fallen but you have learned from their example all the same
- ▪ ....
  ....
- ▪ ....
  ....

ADDITIONAL HISTORY AND BACKSTORY NOTES

Following a trusted friend

- Childhood friends for life
- Your mentor vanished, leaving only cryptic clues
- The spirit of a fallen compatriot spurs you onward
- ....
- ....

Displaced from home

- You still hold a grudge against those who destroyed your old life
- You were separated from your home by disaster
- You earned your banishment and bear that shame
- ....
- ....

Trained for combat but the war is over

- Selling your sword arm beats life on the farm
- The war may be over but you haven't forgotten or forgiven
- You developed a taste for conflict and seek it out to this day
- ....
- ....

GEAR AND OTHER ITEMS OF INTEREST

Whether you're considering the basics, like fifty feet of silken rope plus flint and tinder, or the truly unique, like the enchanted eye of the last green dragon or a hot-rodded custom starfighter, the trappings you carry around convey a story, and that story can be as simple or as complex as your own history. In this section, list your weapons, equipment, and miscellaneous items you possess or have decided to bring with you.

GEAR

Consider the general state of your belongings. Are you a fastidious adventurer who keeps each item organized, clean, and in good working order? Do you let things fall into messy disrepair, counting on good fortune and jerry-rigging to keep your tools useful?

Weapons

Did you begin your adventuring career with the only weapon you'll ever need? A trusted heirloom or sainted magic relic that will see you through all hardship? Or do you replace weapons with the ease of breathing, always seeking the next upgrade? Here, you'll detail your favorite weapons and your relationship to them.

Secondary Weapons

Even the most stringent devotee to the arts of the blade may carry more than one weapon, just in case. Here, list any other weapons you carry or have gathered on the journey.

Weapon (circle one)	Name	Model	Stats and Bonuses	History
primary secondary				
primary secondary				
primary secondary				
primary secondary				
primary secondary				
primary secondary				
primary secondary				

Gear Goals

It's not often that you get the chance to start the game with everything you want, and it doesn't matter if your target is something you need for quest purposes or just a wizard staff you happen to think looks particularly good with your current hat: A large part of adventuring is heading out to get what you want. So, think about just that: what you want. This space can serve as a reminder, a wish list for an interested game master (GM), or just a set of goals to put out in the world.

Item	Description	Probable Location

Gear Relationship

▩ Nothing but the weapons and the clothes on your back
▩ Packed for emergencies
▩ Packed for comfort
▩ Prepared for everything
▩ Compulsive collector
▩ ....

Storage Style

▩ Organized
▩ Untidy
▩ Stored in pouches and straps
▩ Carried by underlings
▩ Stored in otherspace
▩ Kept in the saddlebags
▩ Hidden on yourself

▩ ....

Gear Appearance

▩ Neglected
▩ Piecemeal
▩ Rusted
▩ Stolen
▩ Handcrafted
▩ Heirloom
▩ Store-bought
▩ Polished
▩ Customized
▩ Mystical

▩ ....

TREASURED BELONGINGS

There's always room on your character sheet for the basics, but not every piece of equipment you're carrying is basic. Here you can list the things that have real significance and importance, whether that be to the campaign at large or just to you. Whether it's as simple as a locket with a photo or as epic as the only rock left of your demolished home world, certain items are just more important.

Item:	
Description	Origin
	Birthright Crafted Claimed Reward Discovered Other: Stole .... Purchased ....

Item:	
Description	Origin
	Birthright Crafted Claimed Reward Discovered Other: Stole .... Purchased ....

Item:	
Description	Origin
	Birthright Crafted Claimed Reward Discovered Other: Stole .... Purchased ....

Item:

Description	Origin
	▪ Birthright ▪ Crafted ▪ Claimed ▪ Reward ▪ Discovered ▪ Other: ▪ Stole .... ▪ Purchased ....

Item:

Description	Origin
	▪ Birthright ▪ Crafted ▪ Claimed ▪ Reward ▪ Discovered ▪ Other: ▪ Stole .... ▪ Purchased ....

Item:

Description	Origin
	▪ Birthright ▪ Crafted ▪ Claimed ▪ Reward ▪ Discovered ▪ Other: ▪ Stole .... ▪ Purchased ....

Item:

Description	Origin
	▪ Birthright ▪ Crafted ▪ Claimed ▪ Reward ▪ Discovered ▪ Other: ▪ Stole .... ▪ Purchased ....

PROPERTY

Have you come into possession of something large enough that it requires titles and deeds, as well as maintenance or even a constant staff for upkeep? Perhaps a secret lair, an office for your paranormal investigations, a starcruiser, or a beat-up car that'll get from point A to B if you baby it enough? When you take ownership of conveyance or property, record it here.

Property Type:

- Vehicle/Steed
- Home
- Business
- Town/City
- Kingdom
- Country
- Planet
- ....
- ....

Property Location: ....
....

Description: ....
....

Condition: ....
....
....

Property Type:

- Vehicle/Steed
- Home
- Business
- Town/City
- Kingdom
- Country
- Planet
- ....
- ....

Property Location: ....
....

Description: ....
....

Condition: ....
....
....

ADDITIONAL ITEM NOTES

....
....
....
....
....
....
....
....
....
....
....
....
....
....
....
....
....
....
....
....
....
....
....
....
....
....
....
....
....
....
....
....
....
....
....
....
....
....
....

ABILITIES OF NOTE

As you progress through your game world, you'll become ever more competent at your chosen field(s). Warriors become stronger and more tactically capable; casters add an ever-increasing array of arcane and divine tricks to their arsenal; negotiators become increasingly versed in matters of diplomacy and discussion; and so on. Here you'll record a list of your most efficacious and incredible abilities, along with notes describing how you personalize them to make them truly yours.

SIGNATURE ABILITIES

A perfect blade swing that can cut through the air itself. A softly spoken word that can divert the course of an empire. A granted miracle that calls down heaven itself to cast away the dead. Many characters will come to be known for such incredible feats, and those signature techniques they have will bear their names into legend.

Skill Name:	▨ Physical ▨ Divine ▨ Technological		
	▨ Mental ▨ Social ▨		
	▨ Magical ▨ Artifact ▨		
Skill Effect:	Personal Upgrades:		Element Change:
Increased Range:	Increased Power:		Visual Special Effects:

Power Source (check one):

▨ Innate:	▨ Taught:	▨ Bestowed:
▨ Upgrade:	▨ Other:	▨ Other:

Skill Name:	▪ Physical ▪ Divine ▪ Technological
	▪ Mental ▪ Social ▪ ....
	▪ Magical ▪ Artifact ▪ ....

Skill Effect:	Personal Upgrades:	Element Change:

Increased Range:	Increased Power:	Visual Special Effects:

Power Source (check one):

▪ Innate:	▪ Taught:	▪ Bestowed:
▪ Upgrade:	▪ Other:	▪ Other:

Skill Name:	▪ Physical ▪ Divine ▪ Technological
	▪ Mental ▪ Social ▪ ....
	▪ Magical ▪ Artifact ▪ ....

Skill Effect:	Personal Upgrades:	Element Change:

Increased Range:	Increased Power:	Visual Special Effects:

Power Source (check one):

▪ Innate:	▪ Taught:	▪ Bestowed:
▪ Upgrade:	▪ Other:	▪ Other:

COMPLETE TOOL KIT

Adventurers may make their legacy on the flash and drama of their most powerful tools, but they survive long enough to earn that legacy through growth and maintenance of a suite of survival, combat, and social tools ranging from beginners' survival tools to expert techniques.

Skill Name:	Skill Name:	Skill Name:	Skill Name:	Skill Name:
....	....	....	....	....
Type:	Type:	Type:	Type:	Type:
▪ Technique	▪ Technique	▪ Technique	▪ Technique	▪ Technique
▪ Spell	▪ Spell	▪ Spell	▪ Spell	▪ Spell
▪ Power	▪ Power	▪ Power	▪ Power	▪ Power
▪	▪	▪	▪	▪ ....
▪	▪	▪	▪	▪ ....
Description	**Description**	**Description**	**Description**	**Description**
Stats and Bonuses	**Stats and Bonuses**	**Stats and Bonuses**	**Stats and Bonuses**	**Stats and Bonuses**
Special Effects	**Special Effects**	**Special Effects**	**Special Effects**	**Special Effects**

NON-PLAYER CHARACTERS

Nobody goes through life without making some connections with the people around them, and your character should be no different. Whether it's someone you consider as close to you as a member of your own family, or a simple shop owner that you know has the best prices in town, these are the folks around you that mean the most.

CHARACTER

Character Name: ....

Character Type:

- Government Official/Politician
- Business Owner
- Family Member
- Non-Party Adventurer
- Faction or Gang Leader
- Guard/Soldier
- Refugee/Person in Need
- Old Friend
- Teacher/Expert
- Monster
- Courier
- Child/Youth
- Extraplanar/Extraplanetary Visitor
- ....
- ....

Relationship:

- Friendly
- Transactional
- Competitive
- Adversarial
- Violent
- ....
- ....

Physical Description: ....
....
....
....
....

Character Personality:

- Shifty. Paranoid. Always looking around.
- Boisterous. Welcoming. Calls you "friend."
- Serious. All business. No sense of humor.
- Friendly. Gentle. Likes being helpful.
- Cowardly. Whiny. Hates being called on.
- Gruff. Grumpy. Grudgingly does business with you.
- Greedy. Slick. In it for the profit.
- Flirty. Charming. Makes you feel special.
- Bombastic. Dramatic. All eyes on them.
- ....
- ....
- ....
- ....

What They Can Do for You:

- Has your back in any adventure
- Provides mentorship and guidance
- Boosts your ego with praise and admiration
- Always has the latest gossip
- Buys or sells contraband and rare items
- Knows when big crimes are happening
- Can introduce you to people you need
- Sells discounted goods
- Owes you an undetermined favor
- Gives you a place to crash and lie low
- Can get you the information you need
- Gets anything/anyone where it needs to go
- ....
- ....
- ....
- ....

OTHER CHARACTERS OF NOTE

There are plenty of people in the world that you hear of but don't directly interact with. The name of the local governor that might come in handy lately. The employer who sent you on your latest job. Even the bartender at your favorite hangout might be worth remembering and coming back to. Feel free to jot down anyone that feels important to remember.

ADDITIONAL NPC NOTES

CAMPAIGN NOTES

Herein lies your opportunity to record the great (and the infamous) deeds of your character and their journey. As they grow in power and glory, you'll be able to document each slain foe and each well-met hero on your road, and reflect back on the early days of your starting career. Additionally, it never hurts to keep a record, in case you forget an important name or person who will assuredly crop up later.

PARTY MEMBERS

It's rare that you'll venture forth to adventure alone. Who watches your back? Do you trust them implicitly or do you keep one eye open? You can list the important events and interactions here, or note down the small details to call up again when role-playing in the future.

IMPORTANT EVENTS

How have you made your mark on the world? When the lyricists compose your ode, what stories will they lean on, and what dark paths and mistakes will they carefully elide? Be sure to mention the people you met along the way too, since you never know when they'll turn up again.

BATTLES

There's certainly no reason you can't use this section as a hunting journal or scoreboard, simply listing the types and vitals of every orc or space bug you dispatch. But you might also want to focus on the epic events, the villains that brought you to the edge of doom, or the moments of good fortune or tactical brilliance that make the best boastful brags.

Battle:	Notable Foes	Treasure Acquired
Resolution: ▪ Victory ▪ Defeat ▪ .... ▪		
	Notes and Details	

Battle:	Notable Foes	Treasure Acquired
Resolution: ▪ Victory ▪ Defeat ▪ .... ▪		
	Notes and Details	

Battle:	Notable Foes	Treasure Acquired
Resolution: ▪ Victory ▪ Defeat ▪ .... ▪		
	Notes and Details	

Battle:	Notable Foes	Treasure Acquired
Resolution: ■ Victory ■ Defeat ■ .... ■		
	Notes and Details	

Battle:	Notable Foes	Treasure Acquired
Resolution: ■ Victory ■ Defeat ■ .... ■		
	Notes and Details	

Battle:	Notable Foes	Treasure Acquired
Resolution: ■ Victory ■ Defeat ■ .... ■		
	Notes and Details	

ENCOUNTERS

Not every obstacle on your journey can or will be resolved at the edge of a blade. You might perform some great feat of diplomacy, explore a new and undiscovered land, meet some of the luminaries and famous warriors of your world, or encounter any number of other incredible experiences.

ADDITIONAL CAMPAIGN NOTES

CHARACTER TEN

Character Name

Remember, you can create a character any time, but it takes investment to make them yours. Spend some time thinking about your character—not only their appearance and gear, but also their backstory and their psychology. How will they react in a given situation? This is a great place to start.

CHARACTER NAME AND DESCRIPTION

To begin, you'll detail your character's name and appearance, which is what you'll reference when describing them to other players. Go big and be distinctive! The best characters are the most memorable, and bold decisions when building your look are a great place to begin. And remember: Just because you're starting your game doesn't mean your character only just popped into existence. A few nicknames, epithets, and quirks now will go a long way in the future.

CHARACTER NAME

What's in a name? Potential, for a start. Your character's name can say a lot about them, reflecting their parentage, species, nation, and calling, all while conveying brutality, beauty, or mystery.

Full Name: ....

Known Aliases/Nicknames:

....

....

....

Titles Earned:

....

....

....

Draw your character here:

PLACE OF ORIGIN

Can folks tell where you hail from just by your gait or the cut of your hair? You might be a blank slate or wear your homeland on your sleeve like a badge. If you're looking for inspiration, consider a few of the keywords here.

Place of Origin Name:

....

Location Type:

- Plains
- Forest
- Tundra
- Coast
- City
- Settlement
- Island
- Swamp
- Hills
- Mountains
- Castle/Fort
- Plane
- Planet
- Colony
- ....
- ....

Location Description (check all that apply):

- Shimmering
- Battle-Ravaged
- Silent
- Fetid
- Noble

- Drowned
- Fae
- Calm
- Unsullied
- Stony
- Infested
- Pastoral
- Sunny
- Hardscrabble
- Enchanted
- Bustling
- Burning
- Eternal
- Vanishing
- Dead
- Broken
- Deep
- Whispering
- Forgotten
- Ruined
- Shadowy
- Windswept
- Verdant
- ....
- ....

PHYSICAL DESCRIPTION

You can convey a great deal about your character with little more than body language. Shy and slight, cloaked against the shadows? Or burly and imposing, rattling the ground you walk on? How do you make an impression without a word?

Species/Subspecies:

....

Height: ....

Weight: ....

Build: ....

Eye Color: ....

Body Texture:

- Skin
- Hair
- Fur
- Feather
- Scale
- ....
- ....

Coloring:

....

....

Other Defining Traits:

....

....

....

....

....

....

....

....

....

....

....

....

Defining Physical Traits:

- Battle Scar:

....

....

- War Wound:

....

....

- Striking Feature:

....

....

- Magical Mutation:

....

....

- Curious Affectation:

....

....

- Mystic Special Effects:

....

....

- Tattoos or Scarification:

....

....

- Bestial Attributes:

....

....

- Jewelry and Piercings:

....

....

231

PERSONALITY

What are the day-to-day attitudes that you bring to your party and your work? Are you fun to be around? Honest and headstrong? Select all that apply.

- Pleasant
- Angry
- Morose
- Forthright
- Flamboyant
- Quiet
- Kind

- Reserved
- Outgoing
- Proud
- Selfish
- Devious
- Clever
- Witty

- Guarded
- Trusting
- Suspicious
- Sunny
- Earnest
- Withdrawn
- Lazy

- Meticulous
- Overconfident
- Modest
- Caring
- Fun
- Pessimistic
- Candid

Do you get along well with your traveling companions?

....
....
....
....
....
....
....
....
....

How do you react to strangers and potential foes?

....
....
....
....
....
....
....
....
....

ADDITIONAL CHARACTER DESCRIPTION NOTES

....
....
....
....
....
....
....
....
....
....

HISTORY AND BACKSTORY

Here you'll put into words the past that you've left behind as your character steps forward into the larger world of the game. Does the past haunt you? Are you followed by the remnants of a life you long to escape? Or do you miss the simplicity of the days before you stepped out onto your road? By detailing your history, you provide a map of how you'll interact with the game world now and in the future.

FAMILY BACKGROUND

Everyone comes from somewhere, even if they technically come from no one. Use this space to list your family and their status.

Father's Name: ....

Father Is:

- Living   - Deceased   - Unknown

- ....

- ....

Mother's Name: ....

Mother Is:

- Living   - Deceased   - Unknown

- ....

- ....

Spouse/Partner Name: ....

Sibling Names and Birth Order:

....

....

....

....

Children/Grandchildren Names:

....

....

....

....

....

....

Other Family or Notable Figures' Names:

....

....

....

....

....

What influence did your family have on who you have become?

....

....

....

....

....

....

FAMILY DRAMA

A great way to build hooks and intrigue is to add some family drama that you've left behind or that still haunts you to this day. Check the list items that correspond with your character.

- A sibling fell to evil long ago. You still feel a sense of responsibility when their predation affects those you know.

- You were stolen away from a loving home as a babe and raised secretly for some evil purpose. You still wonder about your original family.

- You're next in line to the throne somewhere, which explains why assassins keep showing up.

- Your parents were replaced by something unnatural when you were small. Somehow you escaped, but you've been weary and perceptive ever since.

- You were raised by a family of another species, leaving you steeped in their culture and a little less comfortable in your own.

- You lost a great love once. You were even considering settling down. But they vanished, and that loss still drives you.

- Your family is a long lineage of a single proud work, but you never had the hands or stomach for the family business. Perhaps they still resent you for abandoning the tradition.

- No childhood trauma befell you or your family. You grew up peacefully and happy, content with your parents and siblings around you. Several are still among us, and you visit them for a source of strength to this day.

- ....

  ....

  ....

WEALTH STATUS

Are you living the high life, or is a rougher path for you at the moment? For some adventurers, this answer can change with ease; they find themselves rolling high after a big score, then scrabble to pay for lodging while seeking out the next job. Here, focus on your character's ideal wealth status. Where on the social strata are they the most comfortable?

- **Contented Pauper:** Scruffy, rough, and cheap even in the best of times.

- **Lean Adventurer:** Always ready to head out; it's always been about the fights instead of the scores.

- **Easy Come, Easy Goer:** You rise to the level money can buy, sleeping in barns with the same comfort as luxury suites.

- **Canny Mercantilist:** Adventure is a second business to you, and you carry wares wherever you go, offering goods and services to towns as you cross them. As such, you're usually comfortable and can expect favorable service and rates from your fellow merchant peers.

- **Savvy Grifter:** You always seem to be comfortable as long as there are enough suckers and marks in the area. The speed of your smile and wit are bested only by the speed at which you leave town.

- **Scion of Success:** Maybe your pockets are empty at the moment, but everyone knows your family has full coffers. Given your vaunted status, it would be unseemly to sleep rough.

- **High Roller:** Money is as important to you as food and water. Even in hard times, you always seem to have the little extra amenities.

- ....

  ....

  ....

HEROIC BEGINNING

There comes a time in every hero's life when they must accept that they are no longer the person they were yesterday—that they can't go back. What did your moment look like? When you stepped out the door and into a larger world, was it voluntary, or were you pushed? In the following list, you'll find a few examples of common steps that take adventurers from an old life to a new one. Choose one or make up your own.

- **Marching to Battle:** You signed up to defend your home, country, or way of life, and marched from home to war. Then you watched someone die and it changed everything.

- **Apprenticeship's End:** It was a grueling education, but even more so an abrupt end, shoved out the door with nothing but the clothes on your back and the rudimentary tools of a trade. You returned home once, but it had vanished from the face of the world.

- **Local Hero:** You weren't trained for it, but when doom befell your home, you rushed to help rather than cower and wait. Now you live for that same rush. However, you were struck by a dangerous curse.

- **Call of the Wild:** You always felt more comfortable away from the smell and noise of the crowd, and the adventurer path gave you the freedom to live outside the walls. You fell in love along the path to adventure.

- **Last Survivor:** You used to be happy, living among your kin in your hometown. But that's all gone now. Unmoored and hardened, you turned to a wandering life. Your simple journey became complicated as you mistakenly stepped into another world.

- **Lying Low:** Your last job didn't go so well. It should've been a perfect score, but the guards had changed, or you didn't see that trap. Now, shamed and wanted, you can't go home, and need to get away with your skin. You found a mystic relic early on, and your fortunes have been shaped around it.

- **An Unexpected Meeting:** You found someone or something in the shadows that offered you a bargain. A short-term job that seems to go on forever, or power at a price. You wonder if you should have said no. You lived when all signs, mystical or practical, suggest you should have died.

- **The Quest:** You set out with a single mission burning in your heart. To vanquish one foe. To retrieve one relic. Perhaps you've yet to do so, or perhaps you've completed that mission, but there are always new quests. You found the first wanted poster with your face on it a day after you walked away from home.

....
....
....
....
....
....
....
....
....
....
....
....

MOTIVATIONS

At a primal level, something calls every adventurer and hero to action. Understanding what drives your character to venture forth every day can help you steer decisions over the course of the game. Choose one of these lists and mark which of the options applies to your character.

- Looking out for the little guy
    - Used to be the little guy
    - Used to be the bully
    - Failed to defend someone in the past
    - ....
    - ....
    - ....
    - ....

- Seeking fame and fortune
    - Left a hardscrabble existence on hope
    - Always felt big things were coming
    - Wants the world to know your name
    - ....
    - ....
    - ....
    - ....

- Called to adventure by the gods
    - You've been chosen since childhood and groomed for this
    - Inspiration came in the form of a vision on the battlefield
    - You've sought out the forgiveness of the gods in atonement for a previous life of transgression
    - ....
    - ....
    - ....
    - ....

- Avenging a wrong
    - It's a personal vendetta the world doesn't know about
    - You seek to stop a great evil that threatens all
    - You already avenged the wrong and are seeking new purpose
    - ....
    - ....
    - ....
    - ....

- A perilous path to power
    - You've made a dark trade, and collection on your debt will come someday
    - The power you've attained came at a dire cost to your body and mind
    - You've left a trail of crimes behind you that you must always run from
    - ....
    - ....
    - ....
    - ....

- Following your hero's footsteps
    - Your hero was the hero of your people— many follow in their footsteps; few succeed
    - Someone saved your life once, and you are compelled not to waste that gift
    - Your hero may have fallen but you have learned from their example all the same
    - ....
    - ....
    - ....
    - ....

ADDITIONAL HISTORY AND BACKSTORY NOTES

- Following a trusted friend
  - Childhood friends for life
  - Your mentor vanished, leaving only cryptic clues
  - The spirit of a fallen compatriot spurs you onward
  - ....
  - ....

- Displaced from home
  - You still hold a grudge against those who destroyed your old life
  - You were separated from your home by disaster
  - You earned your banishment and bear that shame
  - ....
  - ....

- Trained for combat but the war is over
  - Selling your sword arm beats life on the farm
  - The war may be over but you haven't forgotten or forgiven
  - You developed a taste for conflict and seek it out to this day
  - ....
  - ....

GEAR AND OTHER ITEMS OF INTEREST

Whether you're considering the basics, like fifty feet of silken rope plus flint and tinder, or the truly unique, like the enchanted eye of the last green dragon or a hot-rodded custom starfighter, the trappings you carry around convey a story, and that story can be as simple or as complex as your own history. In this section, list your weapons, equipment, and miscellaneous items you possess or have decided to bring with you.

GEAR

Consider the general state of your belongings. Are you a fastidious adventurer who keeps each item organized, clean, and in good working order? Do you let things fall into messy disrepair, counting on good fortune and jerry-rigging to keep your tools useful?

Weapons

Did you begin your adventuring career with the only weapon you'll ever need? A trusted heirloom or sainted magic relic that will see you through all hardship? Or do you replace weapons with the ease of breathing, always seeking the next upgrade? Here, you'll detail your favorite weapons and your relationship to them.

Secondary Weapons

Even the most stringent devotee to the arts of the blade may carry more than one weapon, just in case. Here, list any other weapons you carry or have gathered on the journey.

Weapon (circle one)	Name	Model	Stats and Bonuses	History
primary secondary				
primary secondary				
primary secondary				
primary secondary				
primary secondary				
primary secondary				
primary secondary				

Gear Goals

It's not often that you get the chance to start the game with everything you want, and it doesn't matter if your target is something you need for quest purposes or just a wizard staff you happen to think looks particularly good with your current hat: A large part of adventuring is heading out to get what you want. So, think about just that: what you want. This space can serve as a reminder, a wish list for an interested game master (GM), or just a set of goals to put out in the world.

Item	Description	Probable Location

Gear Relationship

- Nothing but the weapons and the clothes on your back
- Packed for emergencies
- Packed for comfort
- Prepared for everything
- Compulsive collector
- ....

Storage Style

- Organized
- Untidy
- Stored in pouches and straps
- Carried by underlings
- Stored in otherspace
- Kept in the saddlebags
- Hidden on yourself
- ....

Gear Appearance

- Neglected
- Piecemeal
- Rusted
- Stolen
- Handcrafted
- Heirloom
- Store-bought
- Polished
- Customized
- Mystical
- ....

TREASURED BELONGINGS

There's always room on your character sheet for the basics, but not every piece of equipment you're carrying is basic. Here you can list the things that have real significance and importance, whether that be to the campaign at large or just to you. Whether it's as simple as a locket with a photo or as epic as the only rock left of your demolished home world, certain items are just more important.

Item:		
Description	**Origin**	
	▪ Birthright	▪ Crafted
	▪ Claimed	▪ Reward
	▪ Discovered	▪ Other:
	▪ Stole	....
	▪ Purchased	....

Item:		
Description	**Origin**	
	▪ Birthright	▪ Crafted
	▪ Claimed	▪ Reward
	▪ Discovered	▪ Other:
	▪ Stole	....
	▪ Purchased	....

Item:		
Description	**Origin**	
	▪ Birthright	▪ Crafted
	▪ Claimed	▪ Reward
	▪ Discovered	▪ Other:
	▪ Stole	....
	▪ Purchased	....

Item:	
Description	**Origin**
	▨ Birthright ▨ Crafted ▨ Claimed ▨ Reward ▨ Discovered ▨ Other: ▨ Stole .... ▨ Purchased ....

Item:	
Description	**Origin**
	▨ Birthright ▨ Crafted ▨ Claimed ▨ Reward ▨ Discovered ▨ Other: ▨ Stole .... ▨ Purchased ....

Item:	
Description	**Origin**
	▨ Birthright ▨ Crafted ▨ Claimed ▨ Reward ▨ Discovered ▨ Other: ▨ Stole .... ▨ Purchased ....

Item:	
Description	**Origin**
	▨ Birthright ▨ Crafted ▨ Claimed ▨ Reward ▨ Discovered ▨ Other: ▨ Stole .... ▨ Purchased ....

PROPERTY

Have you come into possession of something large enough that it requires titles and deeds, as well as maintenance or even a constant staff for upkeep? Perhaps a secret lair, an office for your paranormal investigations, a starcruiser, or a beat-up car that'll get from point A to B if you baby it enough? When you take ownership of conveyance or property, record it here.

Property Type:

- ▓ Vehicle/Steed
- ▓ Home
- ▓ Business
- ▓ Town/City
- ▓ Kingdom
- ▓ Country
- ▓ Planet
- ▓ ....
- ▓ ....

Property Location: ....
....

Description: ....
....

Condition: ....
....
....

Property Type:

- ▓ Vehicle/Steed
- ▓ Home
- ▓ Business
- ▓ Town/City
- ▓ Kingdom
- ▓ Country
- ▓ Planet
- ▓ ....
- ▓ ....

Property Location: ....
....

Description: ....
....

Condition: ....
....

ADDITIONAL ITEM NOTES

ABILITIES OF NOTE

As you progress through your game world, you'll become ever more competent at your chosen field(s). Warriors become stronger and more tactically capable; casters add an ever-increasing array of arcane and divine tricks to their arsenal; negotiators become increasingly versed in matters of diplomacy and discussion; and so on. Here you'll record a list of your most efficacious and incredible abilities, along with notes describing how you personalize them to make them truly yours.

SIGNATURE ABILITIES

A perfect blade swing that can cut through the air itself. A softly spoken word that can divert the course of an empire. A granted miracle that calls down heaven itself to cast away the dead. Many characters will come to be known for such incredible feats, and those signature techniques they have will bear their names into legend.

Skill Name:	▣ Physical ▣ Divine ▣ Technological ▣ Mental ▣ Social ▣ ▣ Magical ▣ Artifact ▣ ....
Skill Effect:	Personal Upgrades: / Element Change:
Increased Range:	Increased Power: / Visual Special Effects:

Power Source (check one):

▣ Innate:	▣ Taught:	▣ Bestowed:
▣ Upgrade:	▣ Other:	▣ Other:

Skill Name:	▣ Physical ▣ Divine ▣ Technological
	▣ Mental ▣ Social ▣ ....
	▣ Magical ▣ Artifact ▣ ....

Skill Effect:	Personal Upgrades:	Element Change:

Increased Range:	Increased Power:	Visual Special Effects:

Power Source (check one):

▣ Innate:	▣ Taught:	▣ Bestowed:
▣ Upgrade:	▣ Other:	▣ Other:

Skill Name:	▣ Physical ▣ Divine ▣ Technological
	▣ Mental ▣ Social ▣ ....
	▣ Magical ▣ Artifact ▣ ....

Skill Effect:	Personal Upgrades:	Element Change:

Increased Range:	Increased Power:	Visual Special Effects:

Power Source (check one):

▣ Innate:	▣ Taught:	▣ Bestowed:
▣ Upgrade:	▣ Other:	▣ Other:

COMPLETE TOOL KIT

Adventurers may make their legacy on the flash and drama of their most powerful tools, but they survive long enough to earn that legacy through growth and maintenance of a suite of survival, combat, and social tools ranging from beginners' survival tools to expert techniques.

Skill Name:	Skill Name:	Skill Name:	Skill Name:	Skill Name:
....	....	....	....	....
Type:	Type:	Type:	Type:	Type:
▢ Technique	▢ Technique	▢ Technique	▢ Technique	▢ Technique
▢ Spell	▢ Spell	▢ Spell	▢ Spell	▢ Spell
▢ Power	▢ Power	▢ Power	▢ Power	▢ Power
▢	▢	▢	▢	▢ ....
▢	▢	▢	▢	▢ ....
Description	**Description**	**Description**	**Description**	**Description**
Stats and Bonuses	**Stats and Bonuses**	**Stats and Bonuses**	**Stats and Bonuses**	**Stats and Bonuses**
Special Effects	**Special Effects**	**Special Effects**	**Special Effects**	**Special Effects**

NON-PLAYER CHARACTERS

Nobody goes through life without making some connections with the people around them, and your character should be no different. Whether it's someone you consider as close to you as a member of your own family, or a simple shop owner that you know has the best prices in town, these are the folks around you that mean the most.

CHARACTER

Character Name: ....

Character Type:

- Government Official/Politician
- Business Owner
- Family Member
- Non-Party Adventurer
- Faction or Gang Leader
- Guard/Soldier
- Refugee/Person in Need
- Old Friend
- Teacher/Expert
- Monster
- Courier
- Child/Youth
- Extraplanar/Extraplanetary Visitor
- ....
- ....

Relationship:

- Friendly
- Transactional
- Competitive
- Adversarial
- Violent
- ....
- ....

Physical Description: ....
....
....
....
....

Character Personality:

- Shifty. Paranoid. Always looking around.
- Boisterous. Welcoming. Calls you "friend."
- Serious. All business. No sense of humor.
- Friendly. Gentle. Likes being helpful.
- Cowardly. Whiny. Hates being called on.
- Gruff. Grumpy. Grudgingly does business with you.
- Greedy. Slick. In it for the profit.
- Flirty. Charming. Makes you feel special.
- Bombastic. Dramatic. All eyes on them.
- ....
- ....
- ....
- ....

What They Can Do for You:

- Has your back in any adventure
- Provides mentorship and guidance
- Boosts your ego with praise and admiration
- Always has the latest gossip
- Buys or sells contraband and rare items
- Knows when big crimes are happening
- Can introduce you to people you need
- Sells discounted goods
- Owes you an undetermined favor
- Gives you a place to crash and lie low
- Can get you the information you need
- Gets anything/anyone where it needs to go
- ....
- ....
- ....
- ....

OTHER CHARACTERS OF NOTE

There are plenty of people in the world that you hear of but don't directly interact with. The name of the local governor that might come in handy lately. The employer who sent you on your latest job. Even the bartender at your favorite hangout might be worth remembering and coming back to. Feel free to jot down anyone that feels important to remember.

ADDITIONAL NPC NOTES

CAMPAIGN NOTES

Herein lies your opportunity to record the great (and the infamous) deeds of your character and their journey. As they grow in power and glory, you'll be able to document each slain foe and each well-met hero on your road, and reflect back on the early days of your starting career. Additionally, it never hurts to keep a record, in case you forget an important name or person who will assuredly crop up later.

PARTY MEMBERS

It's rare that you'll venture forth to adventure alone. Who watches your back? Do you trust them implicitly or do you keep one eye open? You can list the important events and interactions here, or note down the small details to call up again when role-playing in the future.

IMPORTANT EVENTS

How have you made your mark on the world? When the lyricists compose your ode, what stories will they lean on, and what dark paths and mistakes will they carefully elide? Be sure to mention the people you met along the way too, since you never know when they'll turn up again.

BATTLES

There's certainly no reason you can't use this section as a hunting journal or scoreboard, simply listing the types and vitals of every orc or space bug you dispatch. But you might also want to focus on the epic events, the villains that brought you to the edge of doom, or the moments of good fortune or tactical brilliance that make the best boastful brags.

Battle:	Notable Foes	Treasure Acquired
Resolution: ▨ Victory ▨ Defeat ▨ .... ▨		
	Notes and Details	

Battle:	Notable Foes	Treasure Acquired
Resolution: ▨ Victory ▨ Defeat ▨ .... ▨		
	Notes and Details	

Battle:	Notable Foes	Treasure Acquired
Resolution: ▨ Victory ▨ Defeat ▨ .... ▨		
	Notes and Details	

Battle:	Notable Foes	Treasure Acquired
Resolution: ◾ Victory ◾ Defeat ◾ .... ◾		
	Notes and Details	

Battle:	Notable Foes	Treasure Acquired
Resolution: ◾ Victory ◾ Defeat ◾ .... ◾		
	Notes and Details	

Battle:	Notable Foes	Treasure Acquired
Resolution: ◾ Victory ◾ Defeat ◾ .... ◾		
	Notes and Details	

ENCOUNTERS

Not every obstacle on your journey can or will be resolved at the edge of a blade. You might perform some great feat of diplomacy, explore a new and undiscovered land, meet some of the luminaries and famous warriors of your world, or encounter any number of other incredible experiences.

ADDITIONAL CAMPAIGN NOTES

ADDITIONAL CHARACTER NOTES

ABOUT THE AUTHORS

Jef Aldrich & Jon Taylor are professional podcasters from San Diego. They have been building a podcast brand outside of the big network channels as cocreators and cohosts of the *System Mastery* podcast since 2016, reviewing and commenting on odd classic RPGs and poking fun at obscure stories and systems while taking games for a spin. They each make up one half of the author team for *A Dragon Walks Into a Bar* and *Düngeonmeister*.

THE ULTIMATE BOOKS FOR THE ULTIMATE CAMPAIGN!

PICK UP OR DOWNLOAD YOUR COPIES TODAY!